LOVE IS ETERNAL

Farokh Kharas

iUniverse, Inc.
New York   Bloomington

The views expressed in this work are solely those of the author and do not necessarily reflect
the views of the publisher, and the publisher hereby disclaims any responsibility for them.

iUniverse books may be ordered through booksellers or by contacting:

iUniverse
1663 Liberty Drive
Bloomington, IN 47403
www.iuniverse.com
1-800-Authors (1-800-288-4677)

Because of the dynamic nature of the Internet, any Web addresses or links contained in this book
may have changed since publication and may no longer be valid. The views expressed in this work
are solely those of the author and do not necessarily reflect the views of the publisher, and the
publisher hereby disclaims any responsibility for them.

ISBN: 978-1-4502-7434-0 (sc)
ISBN: 978-1-4502-7435-7 (ebook)

Printed in the United States of America

iUniverse rev. date: 08/3/2011

(An American airlines plane is landing at the J.F.K. Airport in New York, the plane stops, the door opens and the passengers start getting down, along with the passengers walks Helen Lewis with a bag on her shoulder, she is an African woman, five feet seven inches tall, has small black hair, black eyes, a perfect figure, and an attractive round face that has the ability to attract any man, she is dressed in a black suit, with a round neck black t-shirt beneath it, a watch worn upside down on her left hand, she moves her eyes around the airport, and then Helen Lewis says)

"America! That's why they call it the most beautiful country in the world?"

(Helen Lewis walks out of the immigration department towards the airport lobby with her luggage on the trolley and a bag on her shoulder, she comes towards the railing stand where Jane Smith is standing with a paper in her hand that reads "Helen Lewis." Jane Smith is an Caucasian, five feet seven inches tall, with blonde hair, blue eyes, a normal build and a beautiful face, she is wearing a light blue colored knee length skirt, with a blue half sleeved shirt, when Helen Lewis sees Jane Smith holding the sign, she goes towards her, then she stretched out her hand and then Helen Lewis says)

"Hello there, I am Helen Lewis."

(Jane smith smiles, shakes Helen Lewis's hand and then Jane Smith says)

"I am Jane smith, welcome to the United States of America."

(Helen Lewis then gives a hug to Jane Smith and then she says)

"Thank you Jane, nice of you to come and receive me at the airport I appreciate it."

"There is a saying no thank you, and no sorry between friends."

"Ok, but for our friendship's sake, I want to keep the sign paper which you have in your hand?"

(Jane smith gives the sign paper to Helen Lewis and then Jane Smith says)

"Sentimental! I think I am going to get along with you."

"I was hoping for that."

"How was the trip?"

"Just wonderful."

(Jane smith takes the trolley from Helen Lewis and they both start walking, and then Jane Smith asks)

"This is your first time working as a nurse?"

"Yes and I hope I can do it."

"Don't worry Helen; the nurses, the staff and the doctors are very friendly at Get-Well hospital."

(Jane and Helen walk out of the airport lobby)

(Jane Smith and Helen Lewis are in the car, Jane Smith is driving her Toyota, and then Jane Smith asks Helen Lewis)

"Tell me about yourself and your family?"

"I have a mother, a father and eleven brothers and sisters including me."

(Jane Smith is surprised, she smile and then she says)

"Oh? That's wonderful and how is your country Bermuda?"

"Bermuda is a clean and law abiding country and New York?"

"New York is beautiful"

"Great, I hope working as a nurse will be ok?"

"Working as a nurse is hard, sometimes the patients are really nasty."

"I understand, but that's the job we have taken so we have to be very understanding."

"I know that we have chosen this profession, but sometimes it is very frustrating."

"My will power is really strong and I think I will be able to handle the patients."

(Jane Smith Smiles and she put her hand on the shoulder of Helen Lewis and the she says)

"I think I am beginning to like you even better."

"So nice of you to say that."

"Tell me about your family."

"I already told you I have a huge family, but my mother has brought us up very well, she has treated each child equally, my father owns an artificial jewelry shop."

"Life was hard?"

"Not for me because I am the eldest, I pursued a career in nursing so that I can help my brothers and sisters get a good education."

"Self-made woman?"

"No, just practical and following the rules of life, my mother has taught us to be happy with what god has given us, tell me about yourself Jane."

(Jane Smith's face becomes serious, tears fill the eyes of Jane Smith, and then wiping her tears Jane Smith says)

"I was two years old when my father died in a car accident"

"Oh! I am sorry about your father Jane?

"It is ok, but my mother worked hard to bring me up, now my mother lives in New Jersey."

"All alone?"

"No, my mother's sister and her husband live with her."

"Your mother must be missing you?"

"That's life Helen."

"There is a saying that god helps those who help themselves."

"Your way towards life is very positive, well, our apartment has come."

(Jane stops the car; they both get down from the car, Jane Smith opens the back door of the car and takes out Helen Lewis's suitcase, she closes the back door of the car, and then Jane Lewis and Helen Smith walk towards the apartment building)

(Jane opens the apartment door, Jane and Helen come in to the apartment with Helen's suitcase, they come into the living room, Jane closes the door, and then Helen tells Jane)

"Thanks for helping me with the suitcase"

"No thank you, and no sorry between friends, remember? Welcome to our apartment."

(Helen Lewis looks around and then she says)

"The apartment is nice."

"Yeah, two more nurses are sharing this apartment with us, Martha and Rosalie."

"Great, but where are they?"

"They are on duty at the hospital."

"I think I should first go to the Get-Well hospital."

"Relax Helen we will go tomorrow."

"Please Jane, I want to go today."

"Miss perfect, from tomorrow you are joining Get-Well hospital, so rest today."

"My mom has taught me, finish tomorrow's work today."

(Jane gives a hug to Helen and then she says)

"Right miss perfect, as you wish, let's go."

(Helen holds Jane's hand in her hand and they both walk out of the apartment)

(At the reception counter of Get-Well hospital, Wisdom is talking on the phone, the African American man, dressed in a blue janitors uniform is five feet seven inches tall, with small black eyes, a small built, a round face and wavy hair Just like a bird's nest, and then Wisdom says on the phone)

"This is Get-Well hospital.

(At this time Jane and Helen comes near the counter, and then Wisdom says on the phone)

"What's up? Oh? Up there is an operation theatre."

(Jane takes the receiver of the phone from Wisdom's hand, and then she asks)

"May I help you?"

(Jane listens to the other person on the phone and then she says)

"The visiting hours are from five to seven in the evening, you are welcome."

(Jane Smith puts the receiver down on the phone and then Jane Smith tells Helen)

"Helen this is Wisdom, Wisdom this is Helen."

(Helen extends her hand)

"Hello Wisdom."

(Wisdom smiles and then he shakes the hand of Helen and says)

Wisdom—Hi Helen.

(Jane tells Helen)

"Wisdom is a nice person, but his sense and I. Q. is very low."

(Helen looks at Wisdom, and then Helen tells Jane)

"Everyone is not perfect?"

(Wisdom looks at Jane and Helen and then he says)

"I know that?"

(Helen and Jane laugh, and then Jane tells Helen)

"Helen, Wisdom has a great sense of humor, but he isn't really aware of it."

(Helen Lewis looks at Wisdom from head to toe then says)

"They don't make these kinds of people now a day!"

"Yeah, I think god has stopped making people like Wisdom."

(Wisdom is confused, and then he asks)

"They don't make people like me! Why?"

(Jane gives a sarcastic smile to Wisdom and then she tells him)

"One of your kinds is more than enough in this world."

(Wisdom is happy, he smiles and then he says)

"Thank you both for praising me so much."

(Jane and Helen laughs, and then Jane tells wisdom)

"The pleasure is all ours, I think we should move from here Helen?"

"Yes let's go."

(Helen and Jane start walking away, Wisdom looks at Jane and Helen turn from a corner of the hospital, and then he says)

"Woman is the best thing god has made so far, but too understand a woman you have to be a woman yourself?"

(Dr. John Hopes, Dr. Anthony King, Dr. Mike Tyler, Dr. Barry Johnson, Rosalie and Martha are sitting in the canteen having tea and coffee, Jane Smith comes there with Helen Lewis, and then Jane says)

"Hello everybody this is Helen Lewis; she is from Bermuda and joining our hospital from tomorrow as a nurse."

(Everybody says)

"Hello Helen, welcome."

"Hello to all of you."

(Dr. John Hopes is Caucasian; he is five feet ten Inches tall, with brown hair, blue eyes, and a medium built and very attractive face, he is wearing blue pants, a blue shirt and a doctor's white coat over the pant shirt. Dr. Anthony King. is an African American, a strong built and a round face, he is wearing black pants, a white shirt and a doctor's white coat over the pant and shirt. Dr. Mike Tyler is

an Caucasian, he is six feet tall, with blonde hair, green eyes, and muscular built, a long face, he is wearing black pants, a black shirt and a doctor's white coat over the shirt. Dr. Barry Johnson is an African American, five Feet eight inches tall, with small curly hair, black eyes, medium built, and an oval shaped face; he is wearing black pants, a white shirt and a doctor's white coat over the shirt. Jane gets two chairs from a near by table and then she says)*

"Helen, sit down."

(Helen sits down on the chair and then she says)

"Ok"

(Jane sits down on the chairs, and then Rosalie gets up and says)

"What will you two have?"

(Jane tells Rosalie)

"I'll have tea."

Helen smiles at Rosalie and then she says)

"Coffee for me please."

"Ok."

(Rosalie goes away, and then Dr. John Hopes tells Helen)

"Helen is you married or single?"

(Helen tells Dr. John Hopes)

"I am Single."

"Great, what do you think about me?"

(Dr. John Hopes stands up)

(Helen is takes a back by this question of Dr. John Hopes, she smiles and then asks Dr. John Hopes)

"Dr?"

"Dr. John Hopes."

(Helen looks at the face of Dr. John hopes and then she smiles and says)

"Would you mind sitting down please?"

(Dr. John Hopes sits down and asks)

"Now tell me what do you think of me Helen?

(You are an introvert person, very home loving; I can say a straightforward guy)

(Dr. John Hopes smiles and then he says)

"This is not the answer to my question?"

(Helen does not know what to say, she tells Dr. John Hopes)

"When a person wants to climb a ladder he has to climb the first step? Then he has to climb the other steps to reach the top of the ladder? You got the answer to your question?"

(Dr. John hopes tells Helen)

"Diplomatic answer! What about my love life?"

"There is nobody in your love life right now."

(Everybody looks at each other, and then Jane asks Helen)

"Helen, you read peoples faces?"

"Well you can say sixth sense."

(Dr. John Hopes is excited, and then he gets up and says)

"That's great, we need people in the hospital who have a sixth sense?"

"Thank you."

(Rosalie comes with two mugs, puts one mug in front of Helen and one mug in front of Jane)

"Thank you."

"No thank you and no sorry between friends."

"I got this message from Jane a few hours back? By mistake I said thank you?

(Everybody laughs, Helen takes sip from her coffee mug, and then Jane tells everyone)

"It is such a wonderful thing that Helen has eleven brothers and sisters."

(Dr. John Hopes says)

"Hey Helen, you are very fortunate to have so many brothers and sisters, I think the rest of us don't have that big a family?"

"Well you can say that I am fortunate to have so many brothers and sisters and I have very good parents who take good care of us?"

(Rosalie goes near Dr. John Hopes and she asks him)

"If you don't mind then can I ask a question to Helen?"

(Dr. John Hopes says)

"Ok Rosalie you have my permission"

(Again everyone laughs, and then Rosalie asks Helen)

"Where does your father do?

"My father has got his own business, an artificial jewelry shop."

(Martha tells Helen)

"Helen now you have brothers and sisters here also?"

"I appreciate that."

(Dr. John Hopes again stands up and tells Helen)

"Wait, wait, these three men and women are involved with each other, I am the only one who is fancy free."

(Everyone laughs)

(Helen tells Dr. John Hopes)

"I understand your point Dr. John Hopes."

"You better do Helen, because all work and no play make a person?"

"Makes a person mad?"

"That's right."

(Dr. John Hopes takes two roses out of the flower vase on the table and gives it to Helen, and then he says))

"Beautiful roses for a beautiful lady."

(Helen takes the two roses and then she says)

"Thank you Dr. John hopes."

"The pleasure is all mine."

(Everyone looks at each other and smiles)

(In the hospital corridor, Johnny and Susan are looking at each other angrily. Susan is a Caucasian; she is five feet seven inches tall, with shoulder length brown hair, big gray eyes, and a heavily built long face, she is wearing a black colored full-length dress. Johnny is an Caucasian, five feet five inches tall, with small blonde

hair, small blue eyes, and a very small built and a round face, he is wearing a white pant and a white full-sleeved shirt, and then Susan tells Johnny)

"Johnny this is your fault."

"Susan what do you mean by my fault?"

(At this time Jane Smith comes with Helen Lewis, and then Susan tells Johnny)

"Johnny, you are the one who is always fighting with me."

"Susan you are the one who is always trying to find new ways to start a fight with me."

(Susan gets angry and she shouts at Johnny)

"Don't lie."

(Johnny also gets angry and he shouts at Susan)

"You don't lie."

"Shut up."

"You shut up."

(Susan comes very close to Johnny and she tells him)

"Because of you our daughter tried to commit suicide."

"I can say the same to you."

(Jane Smith goes near Johnny and Susan and then she tells them)

"Please, this is a hospital and not your house."

Helen comes near Jane and then she tells her)

"Jane, can I handle them?"

"Ok."

(Helen looks at Susan and then at Johnny and then she tells them)

"Look this is not the time to fight amongst yourselves, your daughter needs the love from both of you."

(Johnny shouts at Helen)

"Love? It is all bullshit."

(Helen in a low voice tells Johnny)

"Mister, love is not bullshit, do you know the meaning of love?

(Johnny tells Helen in a irritating tone)

"Oh? So you know everything about love! Please tell me?"

(Helens becomes angry, she points a finger at Johnny and then she tells him)

"Look mister, until I finish telling you about love, don't interrupt me? Otherwise I will give you a tight slap, ok?"

(Johnny looks at Helen who is really angry, and then Johnny says in a low voice)

"Ok."

"Love is god, worship it, love is togetherness don't separate it, love is children don't abandon them; because love is eternal it never dies."

(Susan's eyes starts filling up with tears, even Johnny's eyes are filled with tears, and then Helen tells them)

"So for the sake of your daughter, please behave like normal human beings, ask people who don't have children of their own, and remember, a child is god's gift to parents."

(Susan starts crying, Johnny goes towards Susan and takes her in his arms and then he tells her)

"I am sorry Susan, please forgive me."

(Susan hugs Johnny and then she says)

"I am also sorry Johnny."

(Helen has two roses in her hand she gives it to Susan and Johnny and then she tells them)

"Take these roses and give them to your daughter and tell her that you are both are sorry."

Susan holds the hand of Helen and then she tells Helen)

"Thank you."

(Johnny also tells Helen)

"Thank you ma'am."

(Helen smiles and then she says)

"You both are welcome, now go into your daughter's room?"

(Johnny and Susan go into the room, Jane puts her hand on the shoulder of Helen and then she tells her)

"Between themselves, they would've never sorted out their differences, Helen you showed them the right way and you were fantastic."

"Jane I was a bit hard on them, but I am happy they understood me."

"Helen we still have more then half a day, let's go and meet my mother."

"That would be wonderful."

"Let's take Rosalie and Martha with us."

"But they are on duty?"

(Jane looks at her watch on the wrist and then she says)

"They both will be off in another half an hour."

"Oh, that's nice."

"Until we wait for Rosalie and Martha let us go to the canteen and have some snacks?"

"Ok."

(Jane and Helen start walking towards the canteen)

(Bob, the canteen owner is making a sandwich, Bob is Caucasian, six feet tall, with long shoulder length golden hair, gray eyes, a heavy built and a big long face, he is wearing a white color long gown, Bob is humming)

"I am a jolly good fellow, I am a jolly good fellow."

(Jane and Helen come near Bob, and then Jane tells Bob)

"Bob, stop admiring yourself."

(Bob looks at Jane and then he looks at Helen and tells Jane)

"Ok, then shall I admire you or your friend?"

(Helen stretches her hand and then she says)

"Hello Bob, I am Helen."

(Bob shakes Helen's hand and then he says)

"Hello Helen, what will you have? Tea? Coffee? Or me?"

(Jane tells Bob)

"Stop giving the old-line Bob, do you want me to call Rosalie and Martha?"

(Bob smiling face becomes serious, and then he tells Jane)

"No, no, I am ok."

(Jane tells Bob)

"That's better, now I want two chicken sandwiches one tea and one coffee."

"You both sit down, I'll bring it to your table in five minutes."

"Let's go Helen.

(Jane and Helen go towards a table and sit down on the chairs, and then Helen asks Jane)

"Jane, when you took the names of Rosalie and Martha, Bob's face went pale? Why?"

(Jane laughs and then she says)

"Bob is a nice fellow, but sometimes he is irritating, one day he asked Rosalie and Martha tea, coffee or me, Rosalie and Martha both caught Bob and started moving their hands on Bob, Bob was taken by surprise and he ran away from the canteen, Rosalie and Martha ran after Bob and you know? Bob ran away to his house."

(Helen starts laughing, and then she asks Jane)

"Then what happened?"

"I had to go to Bob's house to get him here again."

(Helen and Jane both laugh again, then Jane takes out her cell phone and dials a number, she then says)

"Rosalie, get Martha and come to the canteen after your duties are over? We all are going to my mother's house in New Jersey? Ok?"

(Jane switches off her mobile and then she tells Helen)

"Rosalie was very happy, she said she and Martha will come here after their duties get over."

"Great."

(Bob brings a tray with two sandwiches, tea and coffee, puts the sandwiches, tea and coffee on the table, and then he smiles and goes away, Helen tells Jane)

"Bob seems to be a nice guy, only thing he needs is a nice wife."

"He is already in love with a woman who is a widow."

"Then why does he not get married to the woman who is a widow?"

"First problem is that Bob thinks that the widow's husband who is already dead will feel bad and the second problem is that the in-laws of the widow are also not willing."

"Oh! Bob is quite a character?"

"Yeah, he should have been born in the eighteen thousandth century."

(Helen and Jane both laugh, Rosalie and Martha come there, Rosalie is Caucasian, five feet six inches tall, with Shoulder length brown hair, brown eyes, a normal built, and An attractive face. Rosalie is wearing blue jeans, and a Blue t-shirt. Martha is a Mexican, five feet eight inches tall, with black shoulder length hair, black eyes, a heavy built, and a round face. She is wearing blue jeans with a gray color t- shirt, and then Jane gets up and says)

"Helen Rosalie and Martha are here, so we make a move"

"We have to pay bob?"

"He will put it into my account."

(Helen, Jane, Rosalie and Martha walk out of the canteen, Bob looks at them go out of the canteen and then he says to himself)

"If I had not been in love with the widow? I would have married one of them?"

(Jane, Helen, Rosalie and Martha are sitting in the car. Jane is driving the car, Helen is seated beside Jane, Rosalie and Martha are sitting at the back seat of the car, and then Rosalie asks Helen)

"I hope you like it here in New York?"

"Yes I am enjoying it."

(Martha asks Helen)

"What about us?"

"You three are wonderful, but?"

"Martha asks Helen"

"What?"

(Helen tells Martha)

"Martha you and Rosalie should not had done that?"

(Martha and Rosalie look at each other surprised, and then Rosalie asks Helen)

"But what did Martha and me did?"

"Rosalie you and Martha should not had moved your hands on Bob and run after him?"

(All four start laughing, and then Rosalie asks Jane)

"You told Helen?"

(Jane tells Rosalie)

"Yes."

(Rosalie tells Helen

"Helen, you should have seen Bob's face when Martha and I moved our hands on him, he was so afraid, he ran as if a mad dog was after him.

(All four of them laugh again, and then Jane says)

"But Bob is a very helpful person Helen, one day my mother had come to visit me at our apartment and she slipped and fell down, she was bleeding, I was alone at night in the apartment, I called Bob since he lives below our apartment, he came and lifted my mother and ran down the staircase, he then took my mother and me to the hospital; I'll always be grateful to him."

(Helen looks at Martha, Rosalie and Jane and then she says)

"When a person has so much feeling for another person's mother? That person should have a heart of gold? Look from today onwards Bob is our friend; Nobody will harass him ever, right?"

(Jane, Rosalie and Martha nod their heads saying yes, and then Rosalie says)

"Yes Helen you are right"

"And we should see that bob gets married to the woman who is a widow."

(Rosalie and Martha say together)

"Yes we agree"

(Jane says)

"Helen that was nice of you to open our eyes, we should stop making fun of Bob."

(Helen then asks)

"Bob is good looking, any of you did not find him attractive?"

(Jane says)

"I Rosalie and Martha are booked."

"Booked?"

(Martha says)

"Look Helen I am going out with Dr. Anthony King. Rosalie is going out with Dr. Barry Johnson and Jane is going out with Dr. Mike Tyler.

"Oh! That's nice?"

(Jane tells Helen)

"Helen, I think Dr. John Hopes is attracted to you."

"Maybe, but I take my decision on what my heart says."

(Jane Martha and Rosalie ask together)

"And what does your heart say?"

"May be, may be not."

Jane looks back at Martha and Rosalie and then she tells Helen)

"That's a clever answer Helen."

(Every one laughs, Jane stops the car outside her mother's house and then she says)

"Here we are."

(Everyone gets down and walks towards the door of the house, Jane rings the bell, and after a few seconds Jane's mother Carol opens the door, on seeing Jane, Carol's mother hugs Jane and says)

"Jane! So nice to see you?"

(Jane kisses her mother's cheeks and then she says)

"Love you mother."

(Carol kisses the forehead of Jane and then she says)

"I love you too."

(Tears come into the eyes of Carol and Jane, and then Jane says)

"Mother, this is our new friend Helen, from tomorrow she is joining our hospital as a nurse."

(Carol stretches her hand towards Helen and then she says)

"I am Carol, welcome."

(Helen smiles at Carol and then she tells Carol)

"Don't I get a hug too?"

"Oh! Sure."

(Carol hugs Helen and then she says)

"May god be with you?"

"May god be with you too?"

(Carol gives a hug to Martha and Rosalie together, and then Carol says)

"Please come in."

(Jane, Helen, Martha and Rosalie go into the house, and then Carol closes the door)

(Carol Smith is a Caucasian; she is five feet six inches tall, with blonde shoulder length hair, blue eyes, a good figure and a very attractive face, she is wearing a white long sleeved shirt and white pants. Jane, they all come into the living room, Helen, Martha, Rosalie and Jane sit down on the sofa, and then Carol says)

"Let me get you some chocolate donut"

"Mother, where is aunt Stella and her husband?"

"They have gone to Atlantic City to try their luck at the casino."

"Oh!"

(Carol goes away, and then Helen tells Jane)

"Jane you have a very sweet mother"

"My mother is the best mother in the world"

(Helen moves her eyes around the living room and then she tells Jane)

"You have a wonderful house Jane"

"Thanks"

(Martha looks at Helen and then she tells Helen)

"Helen, Jane's mother is very fond of chocolate donuts"

(Then Jane smiles and tells Helen)

"Yeah, and Helen my mother sometimes eats chocolate donuts all day long?"

"Is that so?"

(Rosalie tells Helen)

"Helen, once you eat Jane Mother's chocolate donuts, you will want to eat it again and again?"

(Helen looks at Rosalie and then she says)

"I like donuts too"

(Jane extends her hand towards Helen and then she says)

"Just taste my mother's chocolate donuts Helen and it is a challenge that you will forget all other donuts"

(Helen shakes the hand of Jane and then she says)

"This challenge I will happily except it"

(Carol comes with a tray full of chocolate donuts, and then she puts the tray on the table and then Carol says)

"Finish these chocolate donuts while I get coffee for everyone"

(Jane says)

"Ok mother"

(Carol goes away; everyone picks up donuts and starts eating, after they finish off the donuts, Helen says)

"Nice, very nice"

(Rosalie picks up another donut and then she tells Helen)

"We get donuts in New York also, but they don't taste as good as these?"

"You are right Rosalie, well Jane your mother has got another daughter in me?"

(Martha says)

"Rosalie and I also consider Jane's mother as our mother, so Jane you now have three sisters"

(Jane gets up and hugs Martha, Rosalie and Helen, and then Jane says)

"Great? I love you all"

(Carol comes with another tray with five mugs of coffee, she puts the tray on the table and sits down on the sofa, and then Carol asks Helen)

"How did you like my chocolate donuts?"

"From now on, I am going to call you my mother, I hope you don't mind?"

"Not at all, the pleasure would be all mine"

(Everyone picks up the coffee mugs and starts drinking the coffee, and then Carol tells Helen)

"Helen whenever you miss your mother? Come here and you will get the same love as your mother?"

"Mother"

(Helen's eyes starts filling with tears, Carol puts her coffee mug on the table and then she says)

"Helen whenever tears come in to your eyes, give me a hug"

(Helen smiles and gives a hug to Carol, for a few seconds Helen holds Carol, and then she says)

"I was really missing my mother since morning? I really needed this hug"

"God has stored so much love within a mother's heart, that no matter how much love she gives to another human being, her heart is never empty of love, come I want to hug you all?"

(Helen, Jane, Rosalie and Martha hug Carol, everybody has tears in their eyes, after a few seconds Carol wipes her tears and then she says)

"How about a game of pool?"

(Helen smiles and then she says)

"I love to play pool"

(Carol takes out a ten-dollar bill from her pocket and then she asks Helen)

"Then let's have a ten-dollar bet?"

(Helen also takes out a ten-dollar bill from her pocket and then she says)

"I except your bet mother?"

(Jane says)

"Helen, my mother is a pro?'

"Let's see who is a pro?"

(Carol gets up from the sofa and then she says)

"I love your spirit Helen, let's go"

(Everyone gets up)

(Carol, Helen, Jane, Rosalie and Martha comes inside a room where a pool is there in the middle of the room, they all go near the pool table, the solid and stripe colored balls are set on the table, in between the colored balls is the black ball, the white ball is at the other end of the table, two playing sticks are also beside the table, Helen picks up one stick and Carol picks up the other stick, and then Carol says)

"Helen you take the strike"

"Ok"

(Helen strikes the white ball with the stick, the white ball hits the colored balls, one solid ball goes in to the pocket, it means that Helen has to put the other eight solid balls in to the six pockets of the table, Helen puts another solid ball in a pocket, with the white ball Helen again strikes the solid ball, but it does not go in to any pocket that means that Carol will now get a chance to strike the striped balls, Carol moves her eyes around the table, then carol strikes the white ball with her stick, one striped ball goes in to the pocket, in this way, Carol puts four more striped balls in to the pocket, then Carol misses a shot, Helen gets her turn, Helen puts three more solid balls in the pocket of the table, then Helen misses a shot; now Carol one by one puts four more striped balls in to the pocket, now Carol hits the white ball with her stick, the white ball hits the black ball, it goes in to a pocket, Carol has won the game, and then Helen says)

"You have won the game mother, here are your ten dollars"

(She gives ten dollars to Carol; Carol takes the ten dollars and then she says)

"Helen you are also a good player"

"But mother you are a better player than me"

"If you want you can try again, you might beat me in the next game, you never know?'

"Some other time mother"

"Ok, I will go and put these ten dollars in the box"

(Carol goes away, and then Jane says)

"Helen, mother has a box where she keeps the dollars that she wins, then once a year she gives these dollars to the children's home"

"Oh! That's so kind of her?"

"Yeah, my mother does a lot of charity"

"Does she work?"

"She is in to the candle making business"

"That's nice"

"She has twenty women working for her"

"Jane, from today onwards my respect for your mother, oh, sorry our mother has increased by a hundred percent"

"That's great"

(Jane looks at her watch and then she says)

"The time is four thirty and I think we should go to Manhattan, what do you say?"

(Martha says)

"That's a good idea"

(Rosalie says)

"Yeah, we might not get a chance like this again?"

(Carol comes there, and then Jane tells her)

"Mother, we all are going to Manhattan?'

"No problem, you all carry on but next time you will all spend the entire day with me? Promise?

(Helen, Martha, Rosalie and say together)

"Yeah mother, we all promise"

(Every body hugs carol, and then Helen tells Carol)

"After meeting you, I don't think I am going to miss my mother that much?"

"That's a nice compliment? Thank you? Bye to all of you, god bless"

(Helen, Jane Martha and Rosalie say together)

"God bless you to mother"

(All four go away from the room, Carol is sad, she sits down on a chair, and then tears starts filling up in Carol's eyes)

(Jane, Helen, Martha and Rosalie sit inside the car, Jane starts the car, and then she puts it in gear and drives away, and then Jane tells Helen)

"Helen you are going to love Manhattan, it is the pride of New York"

(Martha tells Helen)

"And we will really enjoy there"

(Rosalie tells Helen)

"Helen, Manhattan is so beautiful that you will want to visit it again and again"

(Helen looks at all the three turn by turn and then she says)

"I have heard so much about Manhattan that I am really excited to see it"

"Jane tells Helen)

"It is a paradise and yeah it is a great place for shopping"

"Shopping! But?"

(Rosalie asks Helen)

"What?"

"I don't have too much money with me"

(Martha put her hand on the shoulder of Helen and then she says)

"We are your friends Helen and all the treats and the shopping is on us, ok?"

"Ok"

(Jane tells Helen)

"Helen, from today onwards what is ours, is yours, only the boyfriends we won't share"

(Everyone laughs)

(Jane drives the car in to a parking lot of Manhattan. Helen, Martha, Rosalie and Jane get down from the car, Jane pays dollars to the attendant, and then Helen asks Jane)

"You have to pay to park your car?"

"Yeah we have to"

(Helen looks up at the tall buildings and moves her eyes around the tall buildings and then she says)

"My god! What beautiful buildings?"

(Martha tells Helen)

"Manhattan is the heart of New York"

"Can we go up on one of this building?"

Jane puts her hand on the shoulder of Helen and then she tells Helen)

"Sure we can go up on this building, but it will waste a lot of our time so we will go next time on this buildings when we come again to Manhattan?"

"Ok"

(Jane, Rosalie, Martha and Helen start walking on the footpath, an old man is sitting on the ground begging for money, Jane, Rosalie, Martha and Helen go near the old man who is sitting on the ground, and then Jane asks the old man)

"Tom, how are you?"

(The old man looks at and then smiles and says)

"Jane! I am fine"

"Tom, this is our friend Helen"

"Another nice looking friend! Hello Helen?"

"Hello Tom"

(Helen extends her hand; Tom takes Helen's hand in his hand and says)

"God bless you"

"God bless you to tom"

(Jane, Rosalie and Martha take out dollars from their pockets and give it to tom, Tom takes the dollars and then he says)

"May god be with you?"

(Jane waves her hand at Tom and then she says)

"Ok Tom, bye"

(Tom waves his hand and then he says)

"Bye"

(Jane, Rosalie, Martha and Helen start walking, and then Rosalie says)

"But first, let's have some fun"

(Three girls are standing with a paper in their hands, written on the paper is)

" Free hugs"

(Jane, Rosalie and Martha go towards the three girls and then Rosalie asks the three girls)

"You three sweethearts, want to earn some dollars?"

"We are hungry for dollars?

(Rosalie points at the papers that the three girls have in their hands and then she says)

"Ten dollars to each of you for your papers for half an hour?"

(The three girls say together)

"Sure"

(Rosalie gives ten dollars to each girl; the three girls give their papers to Jane, Rosalie and Martha and run away, Jane, Rosalie and Martha show the paper to the men who are walking on the footpath, and then Rosalie says)

"A tight hugs free come and get it.

(Martha says)

"On one hug, one hug free from me"

(Jane says)

"Please, the wife and girlfriends turn your faces away and let your men enjoy themselves"

(A boy comes with an I pod in his hand, dancing, Jane also dances with the boy, Jane hugs him and the boy then goes away. A shy man comes and looks at Martha, the man is so shy that when Martha hugs him hard, he gets suffocated and started shouting)

"Help, somebody help?"

(Martha let's the men go, the man falls down on the ground, Helen laughs and claps her hands, and then Jane asks Helen)

"Want to try?"

"No"

(One man comes with his wife, and then the man tells his wife)

"Sandra, please count the floors of this tall building"

(The wife starts counting the floors)

"One, two, three, four, five, six"

(The man goes towards Jane, Martha, and Rosalie and gives a hug to all three of them; he then stands near his wife Sandra who has finished counting the floors of the tall building and then she tells her husband)

"There are twenty floors Sam"

(Sam looks up at the tall building and then he says)

"Is it so?"

"Yes, but why did you make me count the floors of this building?

"I had laid a bet with my friend who was telling me that this building has twenty-one floors and I had told him that it have twenty floors"

"Sam you won the bet?

"Yes Sandra, but you better count it again to make sure?"

"Oh yes"

(Sandra again starts counting the floors of the building)

"One, two, three, four, five, six"

(Sam again comes and hugs Jane, Martha and Rosalie,

(Jane asks Sam)

"What's up my friend?"

"I had laid a bet of hundred dollars with my friend that I can hug all three of you two times"

"Oh! So my friend now gives us our share of fifty dollars or I would tell your wife that you have made a fool of her"

(Sam takes out fifty dollars from his pocket and gives it to Jane and goes away taking his wife, Helen makes an action with her hand and asks Jane that why did she take fifty dollars from the man, and then Jane tells Helen)

"Helen that man was trying to make a fool of his wife and I made a fool of him"

"Tit for tat"

(One well-dressed old man around sixty five years of age comes, and then he looks at Jane, Martha, and Rosalie from toe to the head, then he goes at the back of the three and looks from feet to head, then he comes in front of them and then he says)

"My name is Stewart, I want to marry all three of you, I Have a big house in Manhattan; I have four shops in Manhattan, and after marriage, I'll transfer a shop each on your names, I'll give you each a car also?"

(Jane asks the man)

"What's your age Mr. Stewart?"

"I am only sixty-five years old"

(Martha smiles and tells the man)

"But your manpower must be over?"

"What does that suppose to mean?"

(Rosalie looks at the man from the head downwards and then she says)

"My friend means that we all love children, but with you sir our wish won't be fulfilled?"

"I promise you all that I will produce a child from each of you in one year and if I am not able to do that then I will commit suicide"

(Jane makes a face and tells the man)

"Mr. Stewart we are not interested, so please try your luck somewhere else"

"Are you lesbians?"

(Martha gets angry she grinds her teeth and then she says)

"Mr. Stewart because of your age we are respecting you, otherwise?"

"Otherwise what?"

(Martha moves towards Stewart saying)

"Ok, trying to be over smart?"

(Martha holds Stewart by his collar and says something to Stewart in his ear. Stewart starts removing his blazer, then his Pant, his shoes. Martha leaves Stewart's collar and then Martha says)

"Go and don't look back, or else?"

(Stewart turns and walks away very fast, Jane, Martha and Rosalie start laughing, and then Helen says)

"I thing today is women's liberation day?"

(One man looks at Rosalie and says something to Rosalie in her ear, Rosalie also says something to that man in his ear, and the man starts running, Rosalie starts running after that man. Jane, Martha and Helen laugh and run after Rosalie, Jane, Martha and Helen come running to where Rosalie is standing, and then Helen asks Rosalie)

"Rosalie, why did you run after that man?"

"He asked me in my ear your place or mine?"

(Jane asks Rosalie)

"And what did you tell him in his ear?"

"I told him do you want a kick where it hurts the most"

(Martha asks Rosalie)

"But Rosalie why did you run after the man?"

"He forgot to take his free hug, so I ran after him to give him his free hug? But he ran away into the subway?"

(Helen, Jane and Martha laugh again, Rosalie also laughs, they all go back, the three girls are standing there, and Jane tells the three girls)

"Please take your papers back and yes I have earned fifty Dollars for you"

(Jane gives the fifty dollars to them, all the three girls say together)

"Thank you"

"You are welcome"

(And then Martha says)

"Let's give this blazer, pant and shoes to Tom"

(Martha, Rosalie, Jane and Helen walk towards Tom, they come near Tom, and Martha tells Tom)

"Tom, this is for you"

"Thank you"

(Jane asks Helen)

"Shall we go for shopping?"

"Please?"

(Jane, Martha, Rosalie and Helen go into a women's store. Helen looks at the beautiful tops and then she says)

"What beautiful tops"

(Jane asks Helen)

"Which one do you like?"

"I don't want any tops? I want to send some tops to my sisters in Bermuda?"

(Jane tells Helen)

"Great, you select tops for them, ok?"

"Ok"

(Helen starts picking up tops; Martha picks up a top and then she asks the attendant)

"Changing room?"

"It is at the end of the shop, but you have to wait"

"Why?"

"There is a line"

(Martha removes her top and wears the top she has selected, and then she asks)

"How does it look on me?"

"It looks nice on you"

(Jane and Helen look at Martha, and then they look at each other and laugh, and then Martha tells the attendant)

"I am wearing this top, can you pack my old top?"

"Ok"

(The attendant takes Martha's top and goes away, and then Rosalie asks Martha)

"Do I try my top here?"

"Yes, there are only women in this shop"

(Rosalie removes her top and puts on the new top, and then she asks Martha)

"Does it look nice?"

"Yes, you better wear this top and pack your old top"

"Ok"

(Jane has a top in her hand, Martha looks at her and then she tells Jane)

"Jane you can try the top here like Rosalie and me?"

"I know my size"

(Helen has some tops in her hand, and then Martha asks Helen)

"Helen, wear this tops and see if this tops fits you?"

"I am buying this tops for my sisters and I know their sizes"

"Ok"

(Jane asks)

"I hope everyone has finish shopping?"

(Martha says)

"I am done"

(Rosalie says)

I am also done"

(Helen has some tops in her hand, and then she says)

"I have also got the tops for my sisters"

(Jane says)

"Let's go"

(Jane takes out her credit card and pays at the counter where a lady cashier is sitting; after the lady cashier has swapped the credit card she gives the credit card and a slip to Jane, Jane asks the lady cashier)

"I don't have to sign on your receipt?"

"No madam"

(Jane smiles and tells the lady cashier)

"Oh! As they say nice people no problem in America?"

(The lady cashier smiles back and then she says)

"As they say that the customer is always right"

(All four laughs, then they all go out of the shop with bags in their hands)

(Jane, Martha, Rosalie and Helen are walking, and then Jane asks Helen)

"Helen, the best way to see all of Manhattan is by going sightseeing in the bus, do you want to go?"

"I would love to"

"Ok, let's go"

(Jane, Rosalie, Martha and Helen go out of the store and walk towards the bus, Jane goes towards the man who is selling tickets for the Manhattan sightseeing bus and then Jane tells him)

"Hey Joe what's up?"

"What's up my friend?"

"Can I have four tickets please?"

"Sure"

(Joe gives four tickets to Jane and then he says)

"Here you are ma'am"

(Jane takes the four tickets and gives money to Joe and then she says)

"Thanks"

(Joe counts the money and then he says)

"Ma'am you have paid me five dollars extra.

"That's for you my friend"

"Thanks ma'am"

"No problem, what time does the bus start?

"In just two minutes, you can board this bus"

"Bye Joe and take care?"

"You to ma'am

(Jane, Rosalie, Martha and Helen go in to the bus, they climb the ladder and come on open top of the bus, and then they all four sit down, Helen looks around and then she says)

"Nice!"

(The other passengers come and sit down in the bus, the bus starts moving, Jane takes out a small camera from her pant pocket and then she says)

"Helen, let me take some photographs of you"

(Jane takes Helen's pictures from different angles with tall buildings in the background; Rosalie and Martha then joins in, after that, Jane requests a lady to take photographs of all four, the lady takes the camera, they all four change there positions and the lady takes about ten photographs, and then Jane tells the lady)

"Thank you ma'am"

"You are welcome"

(Then Jane takes the photographs of Helen from the other side, Helen bends down on the floor and Jane takes the Photographs of Helen with the rest of the people in the bus, the guide of the bus comes, he is very ugly looking, short, bald head, and then he says)

"My name is Tommy; I know some people name their dog Tommy?"

(Everybody in the bus laughs)

"Everybody welcome on this bus and welcome to Manhattan, the heart and soul of New York"

(Everybody claps, and then Tommy says)

Tommy—As the bus moves, I will tell you names of the places, anyone wants to ask me a question, I'll be happy to answer it, how many of you are traveling first time on this bus? Please raise your hands?

(Helen looks at Jane, and then Jane says in the ear of Helen)

"Don't raise your hand, because Tommy gives a tight hug and two long kisses to people who are traveling for the first time on this bus"

"He is so ugly looking, I would prefer a kiss from a gorilla but not from Tommy"

"Nobody! Well my bad luck?"

(Helen sees a boy with a guitar in his hand; Helen goes towards the boy and then she asks him)

"Can I have your guitar?"

"Sure"

(Helen takes the guitar, and then facing the people plays a tune on the guitar, Jane, Rosalie and Martha look surprised, then Helen starts singing)

"Love you America, love you Americans,

Love is god worship it,

Love is together don't separate it,

Love is parents don't leave them,

Love is children's don't abandon them,

Love is friendship don't disown them,

Love is remembrance don't forget it,

Love is eternal it never dies.

(After finishing the song, Helen bows her head down everybody claps. Jane, Rosalie and Martha go running and hug Helen, the boy tells Helen)

"You played my guitar so well, you sing so well, but I think to do justice to my guitar, you should sing a lively number?"

(Everybody claps and then they say)

"Yes"

(Helen plays a fast music tune on the guitar, and then she sings)

"Rock, rock, rock, everybody rock,

Dance, dance, dance, everybody dance,

Rock, rock, rock, everybody rock,

Dance, dance, dance, everybody dance.

(All the people in the bus including Jane, Rosalie and Martha get up and start dancing)

"Shake, shake, shake, everybody shake,

"Swing, swing, swing, everybody swing,

"Shake, shake, shake, everybody shake,

"Swing, swing, swing, everybody swing,

(Helen plays a fast tune on the guitar, the driver of the bus stops the bus, gets down and starts dancing, the people on the road who are walking start dancing, the people working in the offices look out of

their office window, they also swing to the tune of the guitar played by Helen, and then Helen sings)

"You are my sweetheart, you are my love,

You are my passion you are my inspiration,

You are my heart you are my heartbeat,

You are my road you are my destination,

You are my duplicate you are my shadow,

Rock, rock, rock, everybody rock,

Dance, dance, dance, everybody dance,

Rock, rock, rock, everybody rock,

Dance, dance, dance, everybody dance,

Shake, shake, shake, everybody shake,

Swing, swing, swing, everybody swing,

Shake, shake, shake, everybody shake,

Swing, swing, swing, everybody swing.

(Helen starts playing the guitar very fast for two minutes, everyone goes wild dancing, Helen stops playing the guitar in the bus, from the building windows and on the road everyone claps, Helen bows her head down twice to say thank you, the driver of the bus sits inside the bus and then the bus moves on,

(Jane is driving her car; Helen is seated beside Jane, Rosalie and Martha are seated at the back seat of the car, Jane asks Helen)

"Helen, I hope you enjoyed your trip today"

"Never in my life have I had so much fun"

(Rosalie hugs Helen and then she says)

"Helen, we all will remember this day, what entertainment you gave us!"

"Sometimes, my heart says that I should let go of myself"

(Martha shows sign of thumps up with he thump and then she says)

"You really rock Helen"

"What about you three! You all three made me laugh my guts out?"

(Jane says)

"Helen, life is too tough in the hospital as a nurse, when we go on an outing like today, we forget everything and enjoyed ourselves"

"Yeah, we should take life as it comes"

(Rosalie asks)

"Helen, what about your love life?"

"My love life hasn't started yet"

(Martha gives a surprised look and then she asks Helen)

"Really! No boyfriends?"

"No"

(Jane looks back at Rosalie and Martha and then tells Helen)

"But without love there is no life!"

"I know, but I have left it to destiny"

(Rosalie gives a kiss on the cheek of Helen and then she says)

"You will find love here, I am definitely sure"

"Hope so?"

(Martha asks Helen)

"What quality do you want in your partner?"

"He should love me more than I love him"

(Jane pats the cheek of Helen and then she tells her)

"God will fulfill your wish"

"I also believe in god, so let's hope for the best?'

(Helen looks at Jane then looks back at Rosalie and Martha and smiles, and they both wink at Helen)

(It is a beautiful morning, Dr. Robert Stanford the in charge of the Get-Well hospital is sitting in his cabin having tea, and Dr. Robert Stanford is an Caucasian, he is six foot two inches tall, he has small black hair, black eyes, and a medium built, he is very handsome; he is wearing a black suit, a dark blue tie and over his suit he is wearing a doctor's white coat, there is a knock on the door, and then Dr. Robert Stanford says)

"Please come in"

(Jane and Helen in their nurse uniform come in to Dr. Robert Stanford's cabin. Helen has a file in her hand, on seeing Jane; Dr. Robert Stanford stands up and then he says)

"Good morning Jane"

"Good morning chief, this is Helen Lewis"

(Dr. Robert Stanford extends his hand and then he says)

"Good morning Helen"

(Helen Lewis shakes hands with Dr. Robert Stanford and then she says)

"Good morning, how should I address you?

"My name is Robert Stanford, but everybody addresses me as chief?"

"Good morning chief"

"Please sit down"

(Jane and Helen sit down on the two chairs opposite Dr. Robert Stanford Chair, and then Jane tells Dr. Robert Stanford)

"Chief, Helen Lewis has been appointed as a nurse by our hospital, she is joining the hospital today"

"Welcome Helen"

"Thank you chief, here are my certificates"

(Helen gives the file to Dr. Robert Stanford; Dr. Robert goes through the papers in the file, and then he says)

"Everything is in order, welcome to Get-Well hospital and best of luck"

"Thank you chief"

"Oh, I forgot to ask you, would you have tea or coffee?"

(Helen says)

"We already had it"

(Dr. Robert Stanford smiles and then he tells Helen)

"Ok then, if ever you want to speak to me, just knock on the door and you are welcome"

"Thank you chief"

(Jane and Helen get up, and then Jane asks)

"Can we take your leave?"

"You can"

(Dr. Robert Stanford stands up and smiles, Helen and Jane smile back at him, and then Jane and Helen go out of the cabin)

(Jane and Helen come out of the cabin, and then Helen tells Jane)

"Our chief is a perfect gentleman"

"Very nice human beings also, let's go to the reception counter"

"Ok"

(Jane and Helen go towards the reception counter where an African American girl named Kai is sitting writing in the register, she is five feet six inches tall, Curly hair, sweet face, black eyes, and then Jane tells Kai)

"Kai good morning"

(Kai looks up and then she tells Jane)

"Good morning Jane"

"Kai, this is Helen, she has joined the hospital today"

"Hi Helen"

(Kai extends her hand; Helen shakes Kai's hand and then she says)

"Hi Kai"

(Jane tells Kai)

"Kai, let me see the duty chart sheet?"

(Kai picks up the duty chart sheet and gives it to Jane, Jane Looks at the duty chart sheet and then Jane and Helen starts walking, Jane tells Helen)

"Helen you have to take the small girl Amana to the operation theatre"

"Amana is being operated for?"

"She has a blood clot in her head"

Helen—Oh my god! Poor thing?

"Amana is just seven years old, you first convince her that the operation is just a minor one so she won't be afraid, her room number is twenty-nine, it's just around the corner, all the best, I will join you in the operation theatre"

"Ok"

(Helen walks away toward the corner; she stops outside room number twenty-nine, closes her eyes for five seconds makes a cross sign on her chest and then Helen enters the room)

(In the room, Amana is lying on the bed looking at her mother and father, Amana's hair is removed, Helen comes in to the room with a smile and then she says)

"Good morning, I am Helen"

(Amana's mother says)

"Good morning, I am samara and this is my husband Morale"

"Good morning to you too?"

(Morale and Samara are both five feet five inches tall, both are African American, both have short wavy hair, both have black eyes.

48

Samara is wearing a brown knee length dress, Morale is wearing a white pant and a white shirt, and then Helen pats Amana's face and says)

"Hello Amana"

"Hello, I am very angry with my mother, she wants the doctors to open my head"

"No, no, Amana listen to me, your mother loves you so much, that's why she has brought you here and mother's love is the best in the world, look I will sing something for you?"

(Helen takes Amana's hand in hers and sings)

Mother o mother, o loving mother,

True love like yours, cannot be found in the whole universe,

You get gold, you get silver, and you get platinum,

But true love like mother, you won't find it in the whole universe.

(Tears come in to Amana's eyes, and then she says)

"Mother please forgive me"

(Samara hugs her daughter Amana, mother and daughter both start crying, and then Helen says)

"I would like to talk to Amana alone"

(Morale takes Samara by the shoulder and they both go out of the room, Helen smiles and then she tells Amana)

"Amana do you feel weak? Are you having difficulty Speaking?

"Yes?"

"Your vision is blurry, sometime you loose your body balance?"

"Yes"

"You get headache, so you can't go to school?"

"Yes"

"Because a blood ball is blocking the movement of the blood in your head, once the blood ball is removed you can speak non-stop, you can play with other children, and you can even go to school?"

(Amana gets up and sits on the bed, and then she says)

"Oh!"

(Helen pats the face of Amana and then she tells her)

"You can even go to picnics with other children of your school"

"Oh wow?"

"Ok, now when you go in to the operation theatre, show the doctors how brave you are"

Amana—Ok, but you will be there in the operation theatre?

Helen—Yes.

Amana—Thank you Helen.

Helen—Come I'll give you a magical hug.

(Helen gives a hug to Amana, Amana also puts her arms around Helen's neck, and then Helen says)

Helen—God is always there with brave people.

(Helen let's go of Amana, then she goes out of the room and closes the door behind her)

(Helen comes out of Amanas room where Samara and morale are standing, Helen tells them)

Helen—You don't have to worry now, Amana is ready for the operation, and I'll tell the janitor to bring a stretcher.

Samara—God bless you.

Helen—God bless you to.

(Helen goes away from there, Samara hugs her husband Morale, and then Samara's eyes are filled with tears)

(Amana is lying on the operation table; Amana's right hand is in the hands of nurse Helen. Dr. John Hopes makes an action with his hand and tells doctor Dr. Tutu to give an anesthesia to Amana, Dr. Tutu asks Amana)

Tutu—My child, are you ready?

Amana—I am ready doctor? What are you waiting for?

(Surprised, everybody looks at each other, Dr. Tutu Gives the anesthesia injection to Amana, Amana is in pain but she looks at Helen and smiles, Helen winks at Amana, Amana Winks back at Helen, the anesthesia injection takes the effect and Amana becomes unconscious, Helen leaves Amana's hand)

(Morale and Samara are standing outside the operation theatre, Samara tells Morale)

"Two hours have passed? I hope the operation goes well?

"Be patient Samara, god is great"

(Helen comes out of the operation theatre; she comes and then she tells Samara and Morale)

"The operation is a success"

Samara looks up and then she makes a Jesus cross sign on her cheat and then she says)

"Thank god"

(Helen smiles and then she says)

"The doctors just opened up the artery and dissolved the clot"

(Samara and Morale hug each other and start crying, and then Helen turns and goes away)

(Martha and Rosalie are having lunch in the hospital canteen, and then Martha tells Rosalie)

"Today is Helen's first day in the hospital and she has duty in the operation theatre?"

"Stop-worrying Martha, Helen is a tough woman"

"I know, but?"

"Everything will turn out ok"

"Hope so?"

(Jane and Helen come in to the canteen, they go and sit beside Martha and Rosalie, and then Martha asks)

"How was everything?"

(Jane smiles and then she says)

"Superb, Helen convinced Amana for the operation"

(Martha and Rosalie get up and they both hug Helen, and then Rosalie says)

"Congrats Helen, Martha was so worried about you?"

(Helen looks up and then she says)

"I think god was very kind to me on my first day"

"I'll get something to eat for Helen and me"

(Jane gets up and goes away, and then Rosalie asks Helen)

"A success on the first day, how does it feel?"

"Great, but before the operation, I had goose bumps all over"

(Rosalie and Martha sit down on the chairs, and then Rosalie tells Helen)

"You know on the first day of my work, I had fainted in the operation theatre"

(Helen says)

"Oh my god!"

(Rosalie says)

"I had to be bed ridden for the full day"

(Helen asks Rosalie)

"What was the operation?"

"It was an accident case, the guy had damaged his skull, and the sight was so horrifying"

(Helen makes a sad face and then she says)

"I also turned my face for a few seconds when the Dr. made a cut on Amana's head"

(Jane comes back and then she asks)

"Bob seems to be very worried?"

(Martha says)

"He was worried about Amana's operation"

(Jane says)

"Well he asked me and I told him that the operation was a success"

(Martha tells Helen)

"Twice Amana's operation was cancelled because Amana's blood pressure had shot up, that is why Bob was tense"

(Bob comes with a tray with two sandwiches on it, Bob puts the two sandwiches in front of Jane and Helen, and then he tells Helen)

"Helen, you did a great job, I was so worried about Amana"

(Tears come out of Bob's eyes, Helen gets up and hugs Bob and then she says)

"Bob, you are a wonderful person, not too many people care about others?"

(Bob has tears in his eyes, he leaves Helen and then he says)

"Today I am not going to take money from you or anybody, everything is on the house"

(Helen sits down and then she tells Bob)

"You will some day make a woman very happy"

"Thank you"

(Bob wipes his tears with his hand and then he goes away)

(Jane say)

"That was so sweet of you Helen to give a hug to Bob?"

(Helens look at Bob who is going towards the counter and then she says)

"Well, sometimes you have to act according to the nature of a person"

(Jane also looks at Bob and then she tells Helen)

"When Amana will start eating, Bob will take bread, Butter and jam for her everyday"

(Helen says)

"Bob has got a heart of gold"

(Dr. John hopes comes there and then he says)

"Helen because of you we were able to do the operation of Amana"

(Dr. John Hopes stretches his hand forward; Helen shakes his hand and then she says)

"You are welcome"

(Rosalie says)

"Dr. John hopes, I think you should take Helen for a candle light dinner?"

"I would love to take Helen for a candle lit dinner"

(Martha asks)

"Helen, Dr. John hopes is waiting for your answer?"

(Helen is a little embarrassed, she looks at everybody and then she says)

"Why don't you all come along?"

(Jane says)

"Helen, now don't be an old fashioned girl"

(Helen looks down and then she says)

"Ok"

(Rosalie says)

"Dr. John Hopes, you better take good care of Helen?"

(DR. John Hopes looks at Rosalie and then he says)

"I will, Helen I will pick you up from your apartment at eight o'clock"

(Helen smiles and then she says)

"Fine"

(Dr. John Hopes gives a flying kiss and then he says)

"I love you all, see you"

(Dr. John Hopes turns and starts walking, Jane says)

"Dr. John Hopes, keep your love only for Helen"

(Dr. John Hopes turns and then he says)

"Point noted"

(Dr. John Hopes goes away, and then Helen says)

"I feel a little shy to go with dr. John Hopes; you all should have joined us"

(Martha says)

"Grow up Helen? Grow up?"

(Everyone laughs, and then Helen asks)

"But isn't it very early to go out with a man?"

(Jane says)

"Look Helen, you know your limits, right?"

"I guess you are right, I know my limits"

(Everyone gets up and then they hug Helen and they go out of the canteen, Bob looks up and then he says)

"God please make Helen and Dr. John Hopes relationship work?"

(Jane, Rosalie and Martha are in their apartment, and then Jane says)

"Helen, please come out, we want to see your dress"

(Helen opens the bedroom door and comes out, Helen is wearing a short beige colored dress, and then looking at her Rosalie says)

(Martha says)

"Helen you look so beautiful in this dress"

(Helen looks at her dress and then she says)

"But is it too short?"

(Rosalie says)

"Come on Helen, you are no more an under aged teenager?"

(Jane smiles and then she tells Helen)

"When Dr. John Hopes sees you in this dress he will be bowled over"

"Seeing me in this dress this he might get wrong ideas?"

(Rosalie says)

"You can always show him his limitation"

(Martha hugs Helen and then she tells Helen)

"Seeing you in this dress, I am getting manly feelings"

"Come on Martha, you are saying this so that I can be happy"

(Helen smiles and then she says)

"You all three are being very kind to me, let me give you all a magical hug"

(Helen gives Jane, Rosalie and Martha a hug each, and then Jane says)

"Helen, when you give a hug, there is a vibratory feeling coming in to our body?"

(Rosalie says)

"Yes! I also felt the same way?"

(Martha says)

"Helen, I think god has given you some inner power"

"God has always been kind to me"

(There is a honking sound, and then Rosalie tells Helen)

"Your man has arrived"

(Martha tells Helen)

"All the best"

(Jane takes Helen towards the door and then she opens and tells Helen)

"Go Helen, and don't be too old fashioned, let your self go today"

"I love you all"

(Helen gives a flying kiss and then she goes out of the door, Jane closes the door, and then Rosalie Says)

"I pray to god to give all the happiness to Helen"

(Martha says)

"Yeah, she is such a caring person"

(Jane hugs Rosalie and Martha, and then she says)

"We pray to god that this outing of Helen and Dr. John Hopes is a success?"

(All three close their eyes and prays silently)

(Helen and Dr. John Hopes are sitting in a restaurant opposite each other, Dr. John Hopes is wearing a white suit and bow, white shoes, a live band is playing, and then Dr. John Hopes asks Helen)

"Helen, what would you like to drink?"

"Orange juice"

(Dr. John hopes makes an action with his hand to a steward, the steward comes and asks)

"Yes please?"

"Two orange juices please"

"Ok sir"

(The steward goes away, and then Helen tells Dr. John Hopes)

"Dr. John Hopes, if you want you can have hard drink?"

"Today, I want to be sizzled by your beauty and not by any hard drink"

"Thank you for your compliment Dr. John Hopes"

"You are welcome and off duty no Dr. John Hopes only John, ok?

"Ok John"

"Thanks"

(The steward comes with a tray, puts two glasses of orange juice in front of Helen and Dr. John Hopes and goes away, and then Helen asks Dr. John Hopes)

"John, you know everything about me, I want you to tell me everything about yourself?"

"I don't want to spoil this lovely moment talking about my past"

"This lovely moment won't be spoiled, I promise you John"

"My father and Mother died in a road accident"

'How?"

"In a bus accident, my parents and I were traveling by a bus from New York to Texas, a drunk man who was driving a car suddenly put a brake to his car, the bus driver tried to put the brake on the bus but the bus over turned, my parents died on the spot, but I survived.

"That's tragic? But who brought you up?"

"My father's elder brother and his wife brought me up"

"Where are they?"

"Five years back my father's elder brother died due to a heart attack and after six months, his wife died of a heart attack too, at that time, we were staying in Texas, I donated their house to a church in Texas, as I had finished my studies, I applied for a job in Get-Well hospital and I got the job"

(Tears fill Dr. John Hopes' eyes; Helen holds both his hands in her hands and then she says)

"There was so much grief in your past life, still you are always cracking jokes and making people laugh?"

(Dr. John Hopes wipes his tears with a paper napkin and then he again holds Helen's hands in his hands, and then he says)

"I have already forgotten the past, now I am only concerned with the present"

"I like your attitude towards life"

"Whatever happens in life good or bad? You should think that god is taking your exam? So you should try to pass in that exam?"

"Your approach towards life is extraordinary"

"Let's forget everything and think about us"

'About us! What?"

"I already have a soft corner for you? What about you?"

"I like life to take its own course"

"Your answer is very diplomatic?"

(Helen takes her hand away from Dr. John Hopes' hands, and then takes a sip of the orange juice and then she says)

"John, please don't rush things, I am a slow starter"

(Dr. John hopes laughs, even Helen smiles; Dr. John Hopes takes a sip of orange juice and then he says)

"Ok, can I ask you to dance with me?"

"Now you are being diplomatic?"

(Dr. John Hopes extends his hand, Helen catches the hand of Dr. John hopes and they go to the dance floor, the music number is slow so they do a slow dance, and then dr. John Hopes asks Helen)

"Can I hold you in my arms and dance?"

"Ok"

"They say that the first step of love starts with friendship'

"Yes, but there are too many steps left for you to climb before reaching my heart?'

"I will keep that in mind"

(Dr. John Hopes and Helen are holding each other tight and dance for sometime, and then Helen asks)

"Are you a family person?"

"What is that supposed to mean?"

"I mean that marry and settle down?"

"From my side, I am ready to marry you right now"

"You can't marry me right now because the church is closed in the night"

(Dr. John Hopes laughs and then he says)

"I like your sense of humor"

"Look John, let's be practical, we both need time to know each other"

"It has to be ok with me, because beggars can't be choosers"

"Never seen a beggar dressed like you"

"Ok, my turn will come to get you back at you when we marry"

"If we marry?"

"Why if?"

"John, we first have to understand each other, then we have to see if we can tolerate each other for life?"

"I will make you very happy throughout your life?"

"Ok, we give each other a year, if in a year every thing is smooth sailing, then we marry?"

"That is ok with me, but what is my limit?"

"We can make love, but no sex, sex only after marriage, do you agree?"

"I agree"

"After marriage, I will go on helping my family by sending them money"

"I will never come between you and your family"

"Do I have your permission to kiss you?"

"It is like asking a hungry man, do you want food?"

(Helen laughs, and then Helen takes the face of Dr. John Hopes in her hands and kisses him on his lips, the kiss lasts for two minutes, Helen takes her lips away from Dr. John Hopes' lips and then she says)

"How was the kiss?"

"Mind blowing, I did not know that the kiss would taste so sweet, from tomorrow I am not going to put sugar in my coffee, I will tell you to kiss me before I drink the coffee"

(Helen laughs and then she says)

"Only when we two are alone? No kissing in front of anybody?"

"Point noted"

"They say that when a person gives something to someone, the other person has to return the favor?"

Dr. John Hopes—Oh!

(Dr. John Hopes kisses Helen on her lips, the kiss lasts for two minutes; Dr. John Hopes takes his lips away from Helen's Lips and then he asks)

"How was that?"

"Out of this world, even the kissing time was the same?"

"I have considered you to be my better half of from today"

"John, your confidence is really great, but if either of us doesn't want to marry after one year, the other won't force him"

"That's just and fair!"

"Another thing, you or me should not interfere in each other life?"

(Dr. John Hopes separates him from Helen's arms, then extends his hand and says)

"I promise"

(Helen's holds dr. John hopes' hand, and then she says)

"I also promise, shall we now go home?"

"Why?"

"I need my eight hours of sleep, otherwise tomorrow I will be upset the entire day"

"What about dinner?"

"Keep it as an excuse, so we can go out again?"

"Your answer has made flowers blossom in my heart"

"But remember that for one year I'll be the only flower in your garden?"

(Dr. John Hopes laughs and then he says)

"My flower, I'll remember that let's go"

(Dr. John Hopes goes towards the table where they were sitting, and then he puts some dollars on the table and walks out of the restaurant with Helen in his arms)

(Dr. John Hopes is driving his car, Helen is seated beside him, and then Dr. John Hopes asks Helen)

"Beautiful lady, do you mind coming in to my arms?"

"I want to reach my apartment safely"

"But I can drive my car with one hand?"

"But your mind and eyes will be on me and not on the road?"

(Dr. John Hopes stops his car outside the Helen's apartment and then he says)

"Good night"

(Helen kisses Dr. John Hopes on the cheek and then she says)

"Good night? Decent dreams?"

(Dr. John Hopes laughs; Helen goes out of the car and goes towards the door of the apartment, opens the door with the key and goes in to the apartment)

(Dr. John Hopes drives away his car)

(Helen opens the door and comes in to the apartment. Jane, Rosalie and Martha are sitting on the sofa with their eyes towards the door of the apartment; and then Helen looks at them and asks)

"You three are not asleep?"

(Jane smiles and gets up, then she tells Helen)

"We were waiting for the Cinderella to return home"

"So sweet of you all to wait for me?"

(Helen comes and sits between Rosalie and Martha on the sofa, and then Rosalie asks Helen)

"Come on tell us how sweet was your experience with Dr. John Hopes?"

"Good"

(Martha holds the hand of Helen and then she asks Helen)

"Good or very good?"

"Very good"

(Jane sits down on the floor opposite Helen and then she says)

"Would you like to share your good experiences with your friends?"

(Helen looks at her three friends and then she says)

"Sure, why not?"

(Jane tells Helen)

"Please, we would like to hear the full experience from the beginning"

(Helen feels a bit shy and then she says)

"First we both ordered orange juice"

(Rosalie, Martha and Jane look at each other surprised, and then Rosalie asks Helen)

"What! Orange juice? You mean to say Dr. John Hopes had orange juice and no hard liquor?"

"Yes my dear friends, Dr. John Hopes had orange juice only"

(Martha says in a surprised tone)

"Whenever he is with us he knocks himself out drinking liquor"

(Helen's smiling face becomes serious, and then she says)

"Dr. John Hopes has had a very bad experience in his childhood, his parents died in a bus accident when he was five years old, but Dr. John Hopes survived the bus accident, he gets drunk in an attempt to forget it this incident"

(Jane, Rosalie and Martha surprisingly look at each other, and then Jane says)

"My god! We didn't know this?"

(Rosalie looks at Martha and Jane and then she says)

"Dr. John Hopes always seems to be a happy go lucky person?"

(Martha says)

"Yes, Dr. John Hopes never even gave us a hint of his past horrifying experience?"

(Helen smiles and then she says)

"Because you people never asked him?"

(Jane holds the two hands with her hands and then she says)

"You are right Helen, we feel really sorry for him, but what was your experience with Dr. John Hopes?"

"Fantastic"

(Rosalie smiles and tells Helen)

"We want to hear it in detail"

(Helen looks at the wall clock and then she gets up and says)

"I think it is too late, maybe tomorrow?"

(Martha holds Helen by her hand and then she makes Helen sit down on the sofa, and then she tells Helen)

"There is proverbs that do tomorrow's work today and today's work right now?"

(Helen sees the eager faces of Rosalie, Martha and Jane and then she says)

"Ok, we went to dance, he asked my permission to hold me in his arms and dance, I said yes, he held me very tight, then I kissed him on his lips, the kiss lasted two minutes"

(Jane, Rosalie and Martha look at one another shocked, and then Jane says)

"What was Dr. John Hopes reaction?"

"He said nothing, so I had to remind him to return the favor; he then kissed me on my lips for exactly two minutes."

(Jane, Rosalie and Martha get up from the sofa, they all three look at Helen with a smile on their faces, and then Helen asks them)

Helen—What?

(Rosalie, Martha and Jane say together)

"I think I hear the wedding bells ringing soon?"

"John wanted to marry me today, but I told him that the church is closed in the night"

(Rosalie, Martha and Jane are shocked, and then Helen says)

"You are looking at me like you three in a shock?"

(Rosalie says)

"You are giving us one shock after another? And calling Dr. John Hopes John?"

"Off duty hours, Dr. John Hopes only told me to call him just John"

(Martha says)

"Helen, you turned out to be a complete surprised package?"

"You three thought that I was an introvert?"

"Jane looks at Rosalie and Martha and then she tells Helen)

"Yes?"

(Martha says)

"I think Helen in your heart, you also have a soft corner for Dr. John Hopes?"

"Yes, you are right Martha, but we have given each other a time limit of one year"

(Rosalie asks Helen)

"One Year! What is that supposed to mean?

"It means that after one year John or me lose interest in each another we will call it quits"

(Jane puts her hand on the side of her head and then she salutes and says)

"Helen, I really salute you?"

(Rosalie says)

"Jane, Martha, from today onwards Helen is our teacher and we are her students? From now if we have any problems with our Dr. boyfriends it will be will be solved by Helen, do you agree?"

(Jane and Martha say together)

"We totally agree"

(Helen gets up from the sofa and then she looks at Rosalie, Martha and Jane and then she says)

"One minute, please understand that I can guide you all? But the final decision will be all yours?

(Rosalie, Martha and Jane say together)

"We three agree"

"Look, this is a bond between you three and I, because if your boyfriends find out that you three are using my guidance, I will be thrown out of my job?"

(Rosalie, Martha and Jane look at each and then they say together)

"We agree, one for all and all for one"

(Helen stretches out her open palm, Jane puts her hand on Helen's palm, Rosalie puts her hand on Jane's hand and Martha puts her hand on Rosalie's hand, and then Jane says)

"Hip, hip, hooray"

(Helen, Rosalie and Martha say)

"Hip, hip, hooray"

(All four then dance moving in a circle saying)

"Hip, hip, hooray, hip, hip, hooray, hip, hip, hooray"

(It is morning, on the reception counter of Get-Well hospital, Wisdom has the phone receiver in his hand, and then he says)

"Ma'am, you have called on a wrong number, yes this is a hospital, but you want Get-Well hospital? No sorry, this is not Get-Well hospital"

(Wisdom puts the receiver down on the phone, Helen comes wearing her nurse uniform, the phone bell rings, Wisdom picks the receiver from the phone and then he says)

"You are talking to wisdom"

(Helen looks at Wisdom surprised, after hearing the words of the other person Wisdom then says on the phone)

"Ma'am, I told you before this is not Get-well Hospital"

(Irritated, Helen takes the receiver from Wisdom's hand and then she asks on the phone)

"Get-Well hospital, may I help you?

(After hearing the words of the other person, and then Helen says)

"Yes, Dr. John Hopes is on duty today up till four in the evening, welcome"

(Helen puts the receiver down on the phone and then looks at Wisdom angrily and then she asks him)

"Wisdom, why did you say that this is not Get-Well Hospital?"

"Because I can't lie"

"You can't lie! What does that mean?"

"My parents have taught me to speak the truth and nothing but the truth"

"Oh my god! Please turn around and read the words?"

(Wisdom turns around and looks at the sign Get-Well hospital, and then wisdom reads it)

"Get-Well hospital"

(Wisdom again turns around and then he asks Helen)

"So what?"

"The lady on the phone asked you for Get-Well hospital and you told her that this is not the Get-Well hospital?"

"Oh! I am really surprised at myself for being so forgetful, but I was working for New York downtown hospital before I joined this hospital"

"That was also a hospital and this is also a hospital?"

"So what's the big deal?

(Helen closes her eyes and controls her temper, then with gritted teeth, she tells Wisdom)

"I am sorry to get into a confused argument with you, now tell me what time is Mr. Mathew's operation?"

"Mathews! Who Mathews?"

(Angrily, Helen takes the daily chart from the desk and looks at it, and then she asks)

"Mr. Mathews was going to be operated for a liver transplant, why is the operation postponed?"

(Wisdom looks right and then he looks left and then he tells Helen)

"Mathews? Oh I get it? Woman problem.

"What do you mean by woman problem?"

"Mr. Mathew son has second thoughts about donating a part of his liver to his father"

"But you mentioned woman problem?"

"Mr. Mathew's daughter in law has stopped her husband from donating a part of his liver to Mr. Mathews"

"Oh! But still I should be prepared for the operation? Where is the material supply room?"

(Wisdom puts his finger on the side of his head and then he says)

"Just let me think?"

(Helen puts her hand on the head of Wisdom and then she tells him)

"I think that you need a brain operation very badly?"

"Is it so? But some people tell me that I don't have brains?"

"I think they are right and I am wrong, I better find the material supply room myself before I lose my brain"

(Helen goes away, and then Wisdom says to himself)

"How can anybody lose his or her brains? Either you have your brains or you don't have your brains?"

(Helen opens the material supply room and goes in, as Helen makes a right turn, she finds Rosalie and Dr. Anthony King kissing, Rosalie looks at Helen with one eye and waves her hand in greeting, Helen smiles and then she says to herself)

"Why spoil their romance? I'll come back later"

(Helen goes out of the room, closing the door behind her)

(Helen is in the corridor of the hospital, she thinks and says)

"I better go and ask Dr. Barry Johnson that what time Mr. Mathew's operation is scheduled for?"

(Helen walks towards the cabin of Dr. Barry Johnson, and then she opens the door and goes in)

(Helen is in the cabin of Dr. Barry Johnson, Helen sees Dr. Barry Johnson sitting on the chair, in Dr. Barry Johnson's lap Is Martha, who has her hands around Dr. Barry Johnson's neck, they are locked in a kiss, and then Helen says)

"I am so sorry"

(Martha looks at Helen and then she asks)

"Sorry! Why sorry?"

"Barging in to Dr. Barry Johnson's cabin without knocking"

(Dr. Barry Johnson smiles and then he says)

"Come on Helen that's ok, as Mr. Mathew's operation is postponed, I was free and even Martha was free, so we thought we should utilize our free time"

(Helen laughs and then she says)

"Excuse me"

(Martha asks Helen)

"Anything important?"

"Just wanted to ask Dr. Barry Johnson when the operation is scheduled for?"

(Dr. Barry Johnson tells Helen)

"I don't know Helen, but can you go and try to convince Mr. Mathew's daughter in law, please? Only then we can go ahead with the operation?"

"Ok, I'll try"

(Helen goes out of the room; Martha puts her hands around Dr. Barry Johnson and then she tells him)

"We should make our love making fast? Because Helen is very good at convincing people?"

"You are right"

(Dr. Barry Johnson kisses Martha's lips hard; Martha moves her hands all over Dr. Barry Johnson)

(Helen moves towards the room where stretchers are kept for the patients, she hears a sound from inside the room, Helen opens the door and hears the voice of Jane saying)

"Come on Mike show me the animal in you"

(Helen is confused, so she silently moves away from the voice; Helen sees that Jane is lying down on a stretcher and Dr. Mike Tyler is over Jane making love to her, Helen shaking her head turns and goes out of the room)

(As Helen goes out she bangs in to Dr. John Hopes, Helen loses her balance but Dr. John Hopes holds on to Helen and then he asks her)

"Helen! That's a nice way to come in to my arms?"

"Dr. John Hopes, please leave me"

(Dr. John Hopes let's go off Helen, and then he asks)

"You came out of the stretcher room? What were you doing inside the stretcher's room?"

"I heard a sound inside the room"

"Then what was the sound?"

(Helen smiles and then she says)

"My friend Jane is playing a love game with Dr. Mike Tyler"

"Oh! Was it exciting?"

"I am only interested in watching baseball games and not love making games"

(Dr. John Hopes holds Helen by her shoulder and then he asks her)

"Then let's start our own love making game?"

"There should be a time and place for the love making game, please tell me what is happening? First I found Rosalie and Dr. Anthony King in the material supply room kissing, then I found Martha and Dr. Barry Johnson in his cabin kissing and now Jane and Dr. Mike Tyler on one another making love?

"Today, the intern doctors and nurses have come to the hospital, they are checking the patients and making reports, so our doctors and nurses are almost free"

"Oh!"

"What do you think Helen?"

"What do I think? What?"

"I mean there are still too many stretchers lying empty inside the room?"

(Helen shows her fists, and then she asks Dr. John Hopes)

"Do you want to get admitted to this hospital on one of the stretchers?"

"I understand your point"

"If your still hot, then I suggest you better take a cold shower"

"Would you be interested in a combined shower with me?"

"That will be only after our marriage, bye and stay cool"

(Helen turns and walks away, Dr. John Hopes smiles and then says to himself)

"Even her no turns me on, what it be like when she says yes?"

(Helen is walking in the corridor of the hospital, a man who is very thin, wearing only a short pant and flip-flops comes running and then he shout)

"Save me, please save me?"

(The man catches hold of Helen and then he says)

"Nurse please save me"

(Helen is confused and then she asks the man)

"Save you from what?"

(Dr. John Hopes sees the man holding Helen, he comes running and then he asks the man)

"Why are you holding the nurse?"

"My wife is after me with a baseball bat to kill me"

(A woman heavily built, wearing a colorful gown, slippers on her feet, comes running with a baseball bat in her hand, and then she says)

"Today I am going to break your thing off"

(The man hides behind Helen and Dr. John Hopes, the woman looks here and there and then she asks)

"Where is the good for nothing shrimp?"

(Helen gets angry and then she tells the woman)

"Please, this is a hospital and not your house, so first stop shouting"

(The woman calms down and then she asks)

"Sorry nurse, but tell me where is he?"

(Dr. John Hopes snatches the baseball bat from the woman and then he asks)

"Now tell me what is the problem?"

"Doctor, before marriage my husband was always ready for action, now before the action he ejects?"

(Dr. John Hopes starts laughing, and then he tells the woman)

"I will solve your husband's problem you go home, ok?"

"Doctor, you better solve the problem or I will smash his thing flat"

"Ok"

(The woman turns and goes away, and then Dr. John Hopes asks the man)

"Now tell me if you are not able to deliver and satisfy your wife, why did you marry her?"

"Doctor, before marriage, I had sex with my wife so many times and it was perfect, now I don't know what has happened to me?"

(Helen asks the man)

"Did you lose the interest and feelings you had for your wife before marriage?"

"Yes, but I still love her very much? What do I do?"

(Helen looks at Dr. John Hopes and then she says)

"Dr. John Hopes, as you can see sex before marriage spoils the relation between the wife and the husband"

"I get your point Helen, ok mister you come with me"

(Helen smiles and then she asks)

"What power are you going to give this man Dr. John Hopes?"

(Helen, your remarks are very taunting but I still love you very much"

(Helen laughs, Dr. John Hopes also laughs, and then Dr. John Hopes making action with the baseball bat like he is playing baseball, and then he goes away with the man, Helen smiles and then she says aloud)

"Trying to be a he man before marriage"

(Dr. John Hopes turns his head and then he tells Helen)

"Love is eternal it never dies"

(Helen smiles and then she says)

"I am making a note of your each and every dialogue"

(Dr. John Hopes tells Helen)

"Want me to buy a notebook for you?"

(Dr. John Hopes turns at the corner of the corridor with the man, and then Helen laughs loudly)

(Dr. John Hopes goes in to his cabin with the man, and then he tells the man).

"Please sit down"

(The man sits down on the chair opposite Dr. John Hopes, and then Dr. John Hopes asks the man)

"How long have you been married for?"

"Six months"

"How many times did you have sex with your wife before marriage?"

(The man tries to think, and then he says)

"After every three days"

"Tell me your feelings toward your wife before marriage and after marriage?"

"Before marriage, I would go crazy if I did not meet my wife in three days and after marriage, on the honeymoon night I could not deliver"

"Now I will get a little personal but don't mind? You were trying to have sex with your clothes on or your clothes off?"

"Definitely clothes off"

"You did not try sex with clothes on?"

"With clothes on! How is that possible?"

"When people want to have quick one, like on the back seat of the car?"

"I don't get you?"

"I mean just your pant down and her pant down on the knees"

"But I never had sex with my wife in a car! We always had sex at home"

"Ok, my questions are finished, you can go down one floor, there you must find dr. Steward Law in his cabin, and he is a sex specialist"

(The man gets up irritated and then tells Dr. John Hopes)

"By mistake, you have become a doctor; I think you should be working in a news channel"

"Why in news channel?"

"Because you ask stupid questions"

(DR. John Hopes is angry but he gives a wicked smile to the man and then he tells the man)

"One more question, does your wife have enough money with her to buy another baseball bat?

(The man is prettified, he says in a low voice)

"Oh my god? I forgot all about her?"

"One more question, do you have enough money to buy a protector for your useless toy?"

(The man asks in a surprised tone)

"What do you mean by a protector for my toy?"

(Dr. John Hopes puts his hand on the shoulder of the man and then he takes him towards the door and then he opens the door and tells the man)

"The cricketers put a safety pad on their toy when they go out to bat? I am talking about the same protector for your useless toy?"

(The man angrily turns and goes out of the door, and then Dr. John Hopes says)

"I should have reminded him that he couldn't replace his useless toy?"

(Jane and Dr. Mike Tyler are making love on the stretcher, their lips locked in a kiss; Dr. Mike Tyler takes his lips away from the Jane's lips and then he asks her)

"Jane do you really love me?"

"No, I am just practicing how to kiss a man"

(Dr. Mike Tyler laughs and then he says)

"Please stop joking and tell me do you love me as much as I love you?"

"Yeah, I love you, but why do you have to ask such a question in the middle of lovemaking?"

"I wanted your answer so that I can ask you to marry me"

"First, we have to be sure of each other so that we can spend our entire life together"

"We are going steady for the last six months"

"I know, but let us wait for sometime, anyway, why are you in such a hurry to get married?"

"I am longing to have kids"

"I am not ready for taking on such a big responsibility"

"Are you thinking about how you will manage work and kids together?"

"I mean I have still not made up my mind"

"I don't understand?"

"Look, I had a very disturbing childhood, I had lost my father when I was two years old, at that time I did not know what a father figure is to a girl, but as I grew up and saw other father's loving their daughters I understood what I had lost in my life, after that I became very attached to my mother, and the love and feelings I have for her right now I can't share them with anyone"

(Tears start coming out of Jane's eyes, she gets up, and then Dr. Mike Tyler says)

"I am sorry Jane if I have hurt you?"

"No, it is not that, I want my mind to be very clear before I take any decision, otherwise in the future; the relationship between you and me might be strained"

"Look, your mother can also stay with us after our marriage or we can go and stay with your mother? Or whatever you say?"

"I don't want a hen pecked husband?"

(Dr. Mike Tyler laughs, Jane also laughs, and then Jane gives a hug to Dr. Mike Tyler and then she says)

"You are a very nice human being, and I truly love you, but after marriage, I will take hourly payment from you?"

"Hourly payment! Why?"

"I always wanted to work on an hourly basis, but here in the hospital, I am getting a weekly salary, so I am going to squeeze you for hourly payment"

"It will be first time in the history that a Husband is paying his wife per hour for making love"

"Yeah, you will be so famous"

"Famous my foot, the other husbands will tear my clothes and make me run nude on the road"

"It will be a great sight to watch you in nude?"

"Come, I will show you my figure now"

(Dr. Mike Tyler tries to catch Jane, but she runs away towards the door, she opens the door and then she says)

"You might need a big leaf to cover your private parts, better buy it from the market"

(Jane goes out and closes the door, Dr. Mike Tyler smiles and then he says)

"Don't worry Jane, I will give the payment"

(Martha is in the lap of Dr. Barry Johnson, they are both locked in a tight hug, and after a few seconds and then Martha asks Dr. Barry Johnson)

"Barry, let's get married? This kind of lovemaking is frustrating for me"

"Martha, please try to understand, I have to pay a lot of money to different people. My father had borrowed the money as he was a gambler"

"But it will be a long time before you pay up the money your father had borrowed"

"Yes I know but I will have to pay them the money that my father borrowed, my father's last wish was to pay up his debt"

"Ok, but we can have sex, right?"

"Sex means kids? I don't want you to abort any kids of mine, as I am an old fashioned guy, kids before marriage is a sin for me"

"I understand your feelings, but you can always use condoms"

"No, sex is a sacred thing for me, I will have sex only when my mind is clear"

"They don't make men like you anymore"

(Dr. Barry Johnson laughs and then he asks Martha)

"What is that supposed to mean?"

"It means that god has stopped making men like you who are men of principles?"

"Is it a compliment or are you trying to pull my leg?"

"I would rather pull your trousers than your leg?"

(Dr. Barry Johnson pulls Martha towards him and gives her a kiss on her lips)

(Rosalie is lying on top of Dr. Anthony King in the material supply room, and then Dr. Anthony King asks Rosalie)

"Whenever we make love, you are always trying to be imposing?"

"How?"

"You are always on top of me?"

(Rosalie laughs and then she says)

"Before marriage, I am the boss so I am on top of you? After marriage you will be the boss and you will be on top of me?"

"Your sense of humor is really great?'

"Tell me one thing Anthony, will our marriage work?"

"Why are you asking me this question?"

"Because we are both miles apart in our thinking?"

"Our marriage will work because I come from a family that knows the value of relationships"

(Rosalie gets up and then asks Dr. Anthony King)

"I always think that you have something hidden in your heart? What is it? Please tell me today?"

(Dr. Anthony gets up and then he says)

"Ok, my mother was the first wife of my father, when my father was in Africa, he married my mother, I was born from her, and then my mother got blood cancer and died, at That time I was just a year old, to take care of me, my aunt that is my mother's sister, married my father, one by one four daughters were born by her; I cannot forget my stepmother's sacrifice, so that's why I want all my stepsisters to get married first"

(Tears fill the eyes of Rosalie; she holds Dr. Anthony King by his shoulders and then she tells him)

"Dr. Anthony King I never knew that I was associated with such a great person, so from today onwards I leave every decision of our lives in your hand"

"Every thing will work out well, I promise you"

(Rosalie hugs Dr. Anthony King)

(Helen is in the hospital game room, she is playing pool on the pool table alone, with the white ball Helen puts five colored balls into the pockets, Jane comes clapping her hands and then she says)

"Helen, you are a good player, but not a very good player, because my mother is the best?"

"I know your mother is the best, but I will be better than her one day"

"My mother says the day somebody beats her in a pool game, she will present her pool table to that person"

"Jane, your mother is a good human being and in my heart I pray to god that nobody beats her in a pool game?"

"Kind of you Helen to say that"

"As much as she is your mother, she is my mother too'

"I saw you coming in to the stretchers room, I couldn't talk you as I was in the middle of making love to Dr. Mike Tyler"

"That's ok, I understand"

"You did not meet Dr. John Hopes today?"

"I met him and he was trying to be romantic but I told him that there is a time and place for everything"

"You really have him on a leash?"

(Helen smiles then put her hand on the shoulder of Jane and they start walking, Wisdom comes from behind and walks behind Helen and Jane, and then Helen tells Jane)

"There is one reason a dog is put on a leash, it means the dog should know who the owner is?"

(Jane laughs loud, and then she says)

"You are too much"

"This is the fact of life, from the start you should show the man who is in control or otherwise he will go out of your hand"

"You are right, I should have thought of this also?"

"Now it is too late Jane, but I think Dr. Mike Tyler is a good match for you"

"Yeah, dr. Mike Tyler is a very understanding man"

"Dr. Mike Tyler is good husband material for you Jane"

"I was going to say the same thing, how is Dr. John Hopes?"

"His past life has been a nightmare for him, he has come up the hard way, but still he is understanding and very loving"

"You think he is the right choice for you?"

"I think so, but?"

"What?"

"It is a wait and watch game with him"

"What does that mean?"

"I myself don't know right now"

"Helen, sometimes you are impossible"

"Look Jane, I try to face facts, not run away from them"

"And sometimes I don't understand you?"

"Life is a puzzle, sometimes you solve a puzzle or sometimes the puzzle remains a mystery"

"Let's go home"

"Ok"

(Wisdom looks at Helen and Jane turn the corridor of the hospital and then he asks himself)

"Life is a puzzle? I think the biggest puzzle on this earth is a woman?"

(Jane and Helen come in to their apartment, and then Jane asks Helen)

"I am making tea for me, shall I make coffee for you?"

"Yes"

"Switch on the T.V. Helen, a very good comedy sitcom love your patients will be coming on"

"Ok"

(Jane goes away, Helen switches on the T.V. On the TV a title comes "love your patients" and then Helen shouts)

"The show has started Jane"

(Helen hears the voice of Jane).

" Helen I'll be there in five minutes "

(On the show two janitors are bringing a patient on a stretcher, they bring the stretcher with the patient near a bed, one janitor lifts the patient by the arms and the other janitor lifts the patient by his legs and throw the patient on the bed, the patient shouts)

"Oh my god, my leg, ah----------ah"

(All the other patients who were sleeping wake up from their sleep, the doctor and the nurse come running hearing the patient's scream, and then the doctor asks the janitors)

"What did you do with the patient? Why did he shout?"

"We just lifted the patient and threw him on the bed"

"Oh my god! I had told you that the patient has a fractured leg? You should have shifted the patient gently on the bed?"

"Oh! We thought you said that the patient had a matured leg?"

(Helen laughs loud; again we show the show on T.V. again they show the same two janitors taking another patient on a stretcher towards a bed, they lift the patient gently and make him sleep on his right shoulder, the patient falls down from the bed on the floor, the patient falls down on the relative who is sleeping on the floor, and then the relative shouts)

"Ah------ah----my head"

(Hearing the shout of the relative, the doctor and nurse come running, the doctor sees that the patient is not on the bed, and then he asks the janitors)

"Where is the patient?"

(The relative of the patient says)

"Doctor the patient is down here"

(The doctor looks at the patient on the floor and then he asks the relative)

"Why is the patient sleeping with you on the floor?"

"He fell from his bed on me"

(The doctor tells the janitors)

"Lift the patient and put him on the bed"

(The two janitors lift the patient and put him on the bed, and then doctor asks the patient)

"Why do you want to sleep on the floor with your relative?"

(The patient tells the doctor in a low voice)

"They put me on the bed on my right shoulder"

"Oh! You two janitors! I told you that this patient's right side is paralyzed; still you laid him on the bed on his right shoulder"

"We thought that you told us that the right side of the patient is sterilized"

(Helen falls down on the floor laughing, they again show the T.V. show, and the doctor asks the janitors)

"You two janitors, where were you working before you joined this hospital?"

"We were working in a garbage company"

"That's why you two have the habit of throwing things?"

(The relative of the patient tells the patient)

"I better shift you to another hospital before these two janitors make me hospitalized also?"

(One janitor tells the relative)

"I know a hospital where they treat one patient free with another patient"

(The relative lifts the patient on his shoulder and runs away from the room, the doctor tells the nurse)

"I think that we should tell the patients that they better take out their insurance before admitting themselves to this hospital"

(The show goes for a commercial break, Helen laughs and rolls down on the floor, Jane comes with two cups and gives one to Helen, and then Jane asks Helen)

"Are you enjoying the show?"

"It is really funny"

(The commercial break is over, on the T.V. They show the doctor is standing beside a patient's bed, the two janitors are also standing beside the doctor, and then the doctor says)

"This patient has been asleep all day! Before that the Patient could not sleep even for an hour?"

(The janitors are sizzled, the doctor looks at the glucose bottle and then he asks the janitors)

"I had given you a white colored glucose bottle, why has the color of the glucose turned brown?"

(One janitor smiles at the doctor and then he tells the Doctor)

"We have put our glucose inside the glucose bottle"

"Our glucose! What do you mean?"

(The second janitor tells the doctor)

"As the patient was not sleeping even for one hour, we took out half the glucose from the bottle and filled it with our whiskey"

"Oh fish! But what did you do with the glucose you took out from the glucose bottle?"

(The second janitor points at the other janitor and then he tells the doctor)

"My partner janitor is always swinging, so I made him drink the glucose for strength"

(Hearing this, the doctor falls down on the floor, and then both the Janitors say)

"We think that the doctor needs the glucose very badly?"

(Helen claps her hands and laughs, and then Jane tells Helen)

"You have really enjoyed this comedy show?"

"I have not laughed so much in my life"

"I think we should put our hospital receptionist Wisdom on the show?"

"You are right Jane? I have not seen a more stupid man than Wisdom?"

"His I. Q. Is very low"

"Low! He does not have an I. Q?"

(Jane and Helen both laughs)

(It is morning, in the corridor of the hospital, Dr. John Hopes, Dr. Mike Tyler, Dr. Anthony King. Dr. Barry Johnson, nurse Rosalie, and nurse Martha, are standing with Mr. Mathew's son Richard and his wife Keith in the corridor of the hospital, and then Dr. Anthony King tells Richard)

"Mister Richard you have to take the decision quickly, your father, Mr. Mathews is not going to last very long without being operated on for liver transplant"

(Richard looks at the room in which his father is there, and then he tells Dr. Anthony King)

"I understand doctor, but?"

(Keith wife of Richard tells her husband)

"No Richard you are not giving a part of your liver to your father"

(Dr. Barry Johnson gets angry and asks Keith)

"But why not! Mr. Mathews is Richard's father?"

(Keith says)

"My husband's father has lived his life and we are just married and it might affect our children when they are born?"

(Dr. Mike Tyler tells Keith)

"Please ma'am let your husband take the decision?"

(At that time Helen and Jane come there, and then Dr. John Hopes tells Richard)

"Mr. Richard, your father is not passing his urine, we have put a tube to let it pass, water is accumulating in his stomach, and if the water reaches his heart he might get an heart attack and die?"

(Hearing the words of Dr. John Hopes, Richard is in tears, and then he says)

"I can't see my father die in front of me, please Keith let me give a part of my liver to my father?"

(Keith gets angry and then she tells Richard)

"No, no, no, if you go through the operation then I will go away to my mother's house and tell my mother what are you going to do?"

(Richard slaps his wife Keith and then he tells her)

"Your mother always interferes in our lives, I am going to go ahead with the operation, and my father has given me birth?"

(Keith starts crying, and then Richard tells the doctors)

"I am ready doctor, let's go"

(Richard goes away with the doctors and the nurses; Helen goes towards Keith and then she tells her)

"Ma'am, as you care for your husband, your husband cares for his father, so please go and be at your husband's side as he needs your support, if you don't stand by him today then tomorrow he will never forgive you?"

(Keith wipes her tears and then she says)

"I did not realize that! Thank you?"

(Helen puts her hand on the shoulder of Keith and then she says)

"Remember god is always with you"

"I will go to my husband? Thank you again"

"You are welcome"

(Keith goes running from there, and then Jane tells Helen)

"You should have been a philosophy professor?"

"But then, I would not have met a friend like you!"

"In words nobody can win with you? Let's go?"

(Helen and Jane are walking start to walk, a nurse named Stella comes out of a room and then she tells Helen)

"Helen, Mr. Mathews is asking for you"

"Helen asks nurse Stella"

"Where is he?"

"He is still in his room"

"Thanks"

"Welcome"

(Stella goes away, and then Jane tells Helen)

"You go inside Mr. Mathew's room, I will just go and see the chart sheet.

"Ok"

(Jane turns and goes away, Helen waits for two seconds outside the room and then she goes inside the room)

(Helen enters the room of Mr. Mathews, in the room are Mr. Mathew's, his daughter-in-law Keith, and on the wheel chair is Amana. Amana was operated for a blood cloth and has a bandage on her head; a nurse is standing behind Amana, Amana smiles and then she says)

"Hi Helen"

"Hi Amana, so nice to see you?"

"Thank you"

(Helen then looks at Mr. Mathews and then she smiles and says)

"Hello Mr. Mathews"

"Hello Helen"

"You called me Mr. Mathews?"

"Well, somebody told me that you are a good inspiration to patients?"

(Helen looks at Amana and smiles, and then she looks at Mr. Mathews and says)

"I just make a kind loving speech that gives patient peace of mind"

"You have to do better than that to me? Because I might die on the operation theatre while the operation is going on?"

"No Mr. Mathews, nothing is going to happen to you"

"Suppose I die during the operation, I want you to put candles on my grave, I always wanted a daughter but my wife died while giving birth to my son, you know god does not always fulfill the wish of a person?"

(Helen eyes are wet with tears, and then she says)

"You called me your daughter?"

"Yes I did, a father would want a daughter like you?"

(Helen starts crying and she turns to go, but Amana stops her saying)

"Hey Helen, you forgot to give your magical hug to Mr. Mathews?"

(Helen turns and runs towards Mr. Mathew, then Helen gives a hug to Mr. Mathews, tears flowing down her cheeks, Helen stays there like this for a few seconds, Martha comes into room and then she tells Helen)

"Helen, it is time for Mr. Mathews to go to the operation theatre"

(Helen takes her arms away from Mr. Mathew's neck, and then she says)

"God bless you Mr. Mathews"

(Helen turns and goes away running from the room, and then Amana tells Mr. Mathews)

"Good luck Mr. Mathews"

"Thank you my child"

(Keith, the daughter-in-law of Mr. Mathews tells her Father in-law)

"Please forgive me if I have ever hurt you?"

"Don't say that Keith, I have no regrets in my life"

(Keith gives a hug and a kiss on the cheek to Mr. Mathews, and then she says)

"May god be with you"

"So many good wishes are with me, now I think I can even fight death"

(Keith makes a Jesus Christ Cross sign on her chest and then she says)

"Amen to that"

(Everyone in the room makes a Jesus Christ Cross sign on their chests)

(Dr. Robert Stanford is sitting inside his cabin, Doris and a boy of four years is sitting opposite Dr. Robert Stanford, the boy is blind; Doris is an African American woman, thirty-five years old, five feet seven inches tall, curly hair, round face, brown eyes, dressed in a white blouse and skirt, Mr. Robert Stanford goes through the reports lying on his table, then Dr. Robert Stanford tells Doris)

"How can anyone save you Doris, the blood cancer you have is at an advance stage?"

"Somebody can give it a try?"

"Doris you know that it is?"

"Please, I want to live for my son?"

(Dr. Robert Stanford looks at the boy and then he asks Doris)

"This is your son?"

"Yes and he has nobody in the world to take care of him? My son is blind?"

(Dr. Robert Stanford is shocked, he then asks Doris)

"Where is your boyfriend Mosala?"

"After my son was born, Mosala just vanished"

"Oh Jesus!"

"Please help me?"

"Doris if you had been in my place? What would you have done?"

"Not lose hope? Because miracles do happen in this world?"

"Doris, what you are saying are only found in books and not in real life?"

"Let's hope against the hope?"

(Dr. Robert Stanford gets up from his chair, and then he walks from here to there and from there to here, and then he says)

"Well today a major liver transplant operation is going on, it will take four to six hours for the donors operation and then it will take six to ten hours for the recipient operation, so I will fix a meeting tomorrow with all the doctors?"

(Dr. Robert Stanford then goes and sits down on his chair, and then Doris says)

"Chief, I am sorry for all the pain I have given you; I was blindly in love with my boyfriend Mosala?"

"Mosala was a Casanova, I tried to reason with you when you decided to leave this hospital, you were the best nurse we had, you did not think for one moment that I who loved you more then anyone in the world and could not live without you?"

(Tears come out of the eyes of Doris, and then she says)

"I had a soft corner for you chief? But you know love is blind? Love does not realize the pain of others?"

"Pain! Till today I am not able to get you out of my heart?"

"As they say, sometimes you win and sometimes you lose"

(Tears comes out of the eyes of Dr. Robert Stanford, he looks at the boy and then he asks him)

"Son what is your name?

(The boy turns his face where Dr. Robert Stanford is sitting, and then he says)

"Robert"

(Dr. Robert Stanford looks at the boy surprised, and then he looks at Doris and asks her)

"Doris you have given my own name to your son?"

(Doris gives a smile and then she tells Dr. Robert Stanford)

"I realized very late that you were a gem of a man? Well only thing I could do was give your first name to my son?"

(Dr. Robert Stanford takes his head in both his hands and then he starts crying)

(Keith is sitting outside the operation theatre on a bench, then she gets up and walks from here to there, again she sits down on the bench, and then Helen comes there and asks Keith)

"Did you eat something?"

"No"

"You better eat something?"

"I don't feel like eating anything?"

"Keith, everything will be all right"

"Almost four hours have passed since they started the operation? I am really afraid?"

(Helen sits down on the bench beside Keith, and then she tells her)

"I understand what is going through your mind? But don't worry; god will make every thing ok"

(Helen puts her hand on the shoulder of Keith, Keith puts her head on the shoulder of Helen, tears rolls down the eyes of Keith, and then Helen tells Keith)

"I will be with you till the operation is over, now just close your eyes and pray"

(Keith closes her eyes and in her mind starts praying, and then Martha comes there and tells Keith)

"Keith"

(Keith opens her eyes and looks at Martha, then Martha smiles and tells Keith)

"Your husband's operation is over and he is just fine"

(Keith gets up and hugs Martha and then she says)

"Thank you, thank you so much"

(Martha smiles at Keith and then she goes away, and then Keith tells Helen)

"You heard, my husband's operation was successful?"

"Congratulations Keith, now please go and eat something?"

"No I will wait for my father-in-law's operation to get over?"

"But it will take at least six to ten hours?"

"I will wait"

(Helen opens her purse and takes out two chocolates and then she tells Keith)

"Please have these two chocolates, because you have to wait very long for your father-in-law's operation to get over?"

(Keith takes the chocolates and then she asks)

"Only if you promise to stay with me?"

"I promise, but after an hour or so we will both go and have a sandwich, ok?"

"Ok, I have no one here in the hospital to support me? But you nurse have stood by me like a sister?"

(Keith gives a hug to Helen, and then Keith looks at Helen and then she says)

"I think you have god inside you?"

"Please, I am just trying to be a good human being, so let me be a human being, ok?

(Keith smiles and opens one chocolate and starts eating the chocolate)

(Jane and Rosalie are watching on T.V. the comedy show love your patients, the two janitors are wearing doctor's coats, one janitor asks the other janitor)

"Now what is the difference between the real doctors and us?"

"No difference, the real doctors are human beings and we are also human beings?"

"Hey why are you swinging so much?"

"I even drank the portion of your liquor?"

"Without drinking, how will I be able to work?"

"Don't worry, leave the important decisions to me?"

(A woman comes running there and then thinking that the janitors are Doctors she says)

"Please help me doctor?"

(The first janitor looks here and there and then he says)

"Doctor!"

(The second janitor tells the woman)

"Ma'am he is a junior doctor and I am the senior doctor, so tell me your problem?"

"It is a private problem?"

(The first janitor smiles and then he tells the woman)

"My senior doctor solves only private problems? Tell him?"

"My husband is a sex maniac, afternoon he comes for lunch he screws me? Then again in the night he screws me? This he does every day? So please tell me what should I do?"

(The second janitor puts his hand on the shoulder of the woman and then he tells her)

"It is very simple, now when you go home and your husband tries to screw you bite his fly off, no fly? No screwing? Ok?"

(The woman is happy, and then she says)

"Thank you for your suggestion Doctor?"

(The woman goes away running, first janitor tells the second janitor)

"What a suggestion you gave to that woman? I think that you must have been a doctor in your previous life?"

"You know why I gave this suggestion to that woman?"

"I don't know?"

"Look, the woman will bite her husband fly off?"

"But what is our gain?"

"After the woman bites the fly? And then the husband won't be able to screw his wife.

"How will it help us?"

"When they want children the husband will come to us for help?"

"What help?"

"He will take our help to screw his wife?"

"You are so smart!"

(The slide on the T. V. comes love your patients, Jane and Rosalie who are watching the show laugh, and then Rosalie tells Jane)

"This show is really great?"

"Yeah, telling the wife to bite of her husband's fly so that the janitor gets the chance to screw the woman?"

(Martha and Helen come in, and then Jane asks Martha)

"Martha, everything went out well I hope?"

"By god's grace the liver transplant operations was successful"

(Jane looks up and then she says)

"Thank god for that"

(Martha sits down on the sofa and then she says)

"Helen was a big help"

(Rosalie says)

"She is a darling"

(Jane and Rosalie get up and they hug Helen, and then Helen says)

"And you all are my darlings?"

(Martha asks)

"Please can we have some food?"

(Jane says)

"Yeah, the food is ready on the dining table, let's eat?'

(Jane, Rosalie, Martha and Helen go towards the dining table, they sit down on the chairs, Jane serves food to all, and then Martha says)

"Tomorrow morning there is a meeting in the hall"

(Rosalie asks)

"What meeting?"

"Chief has called the meeting; all the doctors and nurses on our floor have to attend the meeting"

(Jane says)

"Looks like something serious?"

Martha—Yes! The first time I have seen the chief looking so sad.

(All the four pray to god silently, they make a Jesus Christ Cross sign on their chests and then they open their eyes and start eating the food)

(It is morning, Dr. Robert Stanford, Doris her son Robert are standing opposite Dr. John Hopes, Dr. Barry Johnson, Dr. Anthony King, Dr. Mike Tyler, nurse Jane, nurse Helen, nurse Rosalie, and nurse Martha, and then Dr. Robert Stanford says)

"I don't want to waste time in formalities, because what I am going to tell you are very important, the lady beside me is Doris who is at the advance stage of blood cancer, I want to save her for my personal reason, look I don't want anybody to tell me that this case of blood cancer is not possible to cure or that Doris has less chance of survival? Even I don't want to hear from you all that we will try our best to save Doris? Now I want to clear everything, I was in love with Doris when she was working for this hospital as a nurse, but Doris loved a man called Mosala, Doris left this hospital five years back, she has her son standing beside her, he is blind and his name is Robert"

(Hearing the word Robert everybody looks at each other, and then they look at Dr. Robert Stanford, and then Dr. Robert Stanford says)

"You all are confused by this boy's name Robert? But I want to say that the name is the only identification with me? This boy belongs to Doris and her boyfriend Mosala, I want her admitted today in this hospital, you can put her name as Doris Stanford"

(Everyone looks at each other surprised, and then Dr. Robert Stanford asks)

"Any questions?"

(Dr. John Hopes smiles and then he says)

"Chief, we are all very happy that you have so much trust in us and we won't let your trust down, but for Doris case we might have to take help of other doctors from other hospitals?"

(Dr. Robert Stanford can hardly say the words)

"I don't mind? But please help Doris fight for her life?"

(Tears comes out of the eyes of Doris, Dr. Robert Stanford puts his hand on the shoulder of Doris, and then Dr. Robert Stanford says in a chocking voice)

"More than medicine Doris needs the prayers, blessings and support from you all?"

(There is silence in the room for ten seconds, nobody knows what to do or what to say, they had never seen the chief in such an emotional turmoil, Helen goes towards Doris and then she puts her hand on the shoulder of Doris and then she tells her)

"Doris, this is not your fight alone? We all are there with you to fight your battle?"

(Doris kisses the hand of Helen and then she says)

"I appreciate it"

(Helen tells Doris)

"Let's go?"

(Helen takes Doris away; everyone goes away, Dr. Robert Stanford takes the hand of Robert in his hand and then he says)

"From today onwards you can call me father, what?"

"Father"

"That's it"

(Dr. John Hopes, Dr. Barry Johnson, Dr. Anthony King, Dr. Mike Tyler are in the cabin of Dr. John Hopes, and then Dr. Barry Johnson says)

"In my career at this hospital I have never seen our chief so helpless?"

(Dr. Anthony King says)

"Love Dr. Barry Johnson? Love has no boundaries?"

(Dr. Mike Tyler looks at everyone and then he says)

"What our chief has asked us to do is not possible?"

(Dr. John Hopes says)

"We all know that we will be fighting a losing battle trying to save Doris? But we should all give our best and let god decide the fate? The first thing we do is call up Dr. Peter Liao from Manhattan hospital, the second thing we do is call up Dr. Steve Wayne from downtown Hospital, they both are the specialists for blood cancer"

(Dr. John Hopes looks at the other three doctors, they all shake their heads in saying yes, Dr. John hopes takes out his mobile and dials a number, he waits and then Dr. John Hopes says)

"Is this Dr. Peter Liao?"

(Dr. John hopes hears the voice from the other side)

"Yes"

"Good morning Dr. Peter Liao? This is Dr. John Hopes from the Get-Well hospital"

(Dr. John hopes hears the voice from other side)

"Good morning Dr. john Hopes"

"We need your help for a cancer patient, if it is possible then can you come right now to Get-Well hospital? It is an emergency?"

(Dr. John Hopes hears the voice from the other side)

"Ok, I will be there in an hour, thanks for calling me Dr. John Hopes and have a nice day"

"Thank you Dr. Peter Liao"

(Dr. John Hopes switches off the mobile, and then he says)

"Dr. Peter Liao will be here in an hour, so let's make the arrangements, Dr. Mike Tyler please call Dr. Steve Wayne from the downtown hospital, as he is your friend?"

(Dr. Mike Tyler says)

"I'll call him for sure"

(Dr. John Hopes looks at everyone and then he asks)

"Any suggestions?"

(Dr. Barry Johnson says)

"No, we go ahead with what you say?"

(Dr. Anthony King says)

"Yes, I also agree"

(Dr. John Hopes is almost in tears and then he says)

"We all hope that love wins over death?"

(Doris is in the hospital room sitting on the bed reading a book titled "can you turn the clock back" Helen comes in to the room with a rose in her hand, and then she tells Doris)

"Hi Doris"

(Doris puts the book on the bed and then she says)

"Hi Helen, nice to see you"

(Helen gives the flower to Doris and then she says)

"Like this rose your life will also bloom and one day your life will be full of happiness"

"Sweet of you to say that"

(Doris takes the rose and then Helen tells Doris)

"Now guess who has come to meet you?"

(Doris tries to guess, and then she says)

"I don't think I am good at guessing names?"

9Helen looks at the door and then she says)

"Please come in?"

(From the door Bob comes in with a bagel and a cup of coffee, and then Bob says)

"What's up Doris?"

(Doris says)

"Bob! It is a pleasure to see you?"

(Bob says)

"The pleasure is all mine"

(Bob puts the tray on the bed, Doris gives a hug to Bob, Bob has tears in his eyes, and then he says)

"You even forgot your namesake brother?"

(Tears fall from the eyes of Doris and then she says)

"No Bob, no, how can I forget a brother like you"

(Helen is in tears, she wipes her tears, and then Bob tells Doris)

"Look I have brought everything in bagel with butter and coffee?"

"Oh! You still remember?"

"You have always been a warm person, how can I forget?"

"Bob, I really love you"

"At least you could have called me when Mosala left you high and dry?"

"At that time I was not in my senses Bob"

"I have never hurt a fly in my life? But if ever I get my hands on Mosala I'll wring his neck?"

"Well, it was my fault to trust him?"

"You were always a strong person Doris?'

"I know Bob, but everyone makes a mistake?'

"Ok, I understand, please eat this bagel and remember everyday the breakfast is on me?"

"What about lunch and dinner Bob?"

(Bob smiles and then he tells Doris)

"Your loyal lover the chief is there to take care of your lunch and dinner?"

(Everyone laughs, Doris starts eating, tears starts falling from the eyes of Bob, he goes out of the room, and then Doris asks Helen)

"Helen, do you think I have a chance?"

"Yes Doris, right now a meeting is going between the doctors, but Doris you have to make your will power very strong?"

"I will fight till my last breath"

"That's the spirit Doris, I'll make a move? As I have to see other patients also? And yes from today onwards your treatment might start? You may remain unconscious so let me give you the magical hug?"

(Helen gives a hug to Doris, and then she turns and walks towards the door, Helen turns and looks at Doris and gives Doris a flying kiss, Doris also gives a flying kiss to Helen, then Helen goes out of the door, Doris looks up and then she says)

"God please help me in my fight to fight my death"

(Dr. Robert Stanford, Dr. John hopes, Dr. Barry Johnson, Dr. Anthony King, Dr. Mike Tyler is sitting in the conference room on the right side, Dr. Peter Liao and Dr. Steve Wayne are sitting on the left side of the conference room studying the reports of Doris, Dr. Peter Liao is a Chinese, five feet six inches tall, has a round face, brown eyes, black hair, is wearing a gray suit with a dark blue tie, and is about forty-five years of age, Dr. Steve Wayne is a giant, six foot two inches tall, brown short hair, very handsome face like a movie star, wearing a black suit and a black tie, and has blue eyes, Dr. Peter Liao and Dr. Steve Wayne discuss among themselves in a low voice, they discuss for five minutes, and then Dr. Peter Liao says)

"Dr. Steve Wayne and I have discussed and have come to a decision that the patient Doris has to under go Radioimmunotherapy treatment, this treatment of Radioimmunotherapy works by directing specifocally engineered antibodies to deliver tiny but effective doses of Radiation directly to cancer cells, Radiation treatment can harm surrounding tissues despite our best attempts to focus the beam, this is a theory research by university researcher Dr. Daniel Vallera, so?

(Dr. Robert Stanford says)

"We all have full trust in your judgment Dr. Peter Liao and Dr. Steve Wayne, you two is the best judge; we leave everything in your hands"

Dr. Steve Wayne— In any treatment the risks are there for the patient to have side effects, but the results are extremely promising and it has completely eradicate the cancer cells grafted in mice?"

(Dr. Robert Stanford looks at everyone and then he says)

"That's great hope for Doris?"

(Dr. Peter Liao says)

"We are very positive about this treatment, rest we leave it to god?'

(Dr. Steve Wayne says)

"After twenty-four hours we start the treatment, but we both will be back in five hours and start working on the patient"

(Dr. Robert Stanford says)

"I appreciate it"

(Dr. Peter Liao and Dr. Steve Wayne shake hands with all the other doctors, and then Dr. Robert Stanford tells them)

"This way please?"

(Dr. Peter Liao and Dr. Steve Wayne go with Dr. Robert Stanford, and then Dr. John Hopes says)

"If mice responded to this treatment then I think this treatment is going to work on Doris?"

(Dr. Anthony King says)

"Yes I agree with Dr. John Hopes? This is the most safe and effective treatment?"

(Dr. Barry Johnson says)

"And this treatment is the only hope for Doris?"

(Dr. Mike Tyler says)

(Dr. Peter Liao and Dr. Steve Wayne are the two best doctors for blood cancer in New York and they are famous all over the world? In my heart I feel that a miracle is going to take place?"

(Dr. John Hopes says)

"They say love always wins in the end? And so many prayers are with Doris?"

(Dr. John Hopes makes the sign of the Jesus Christ Cross on his chest and then he says)

"In the name of the father, the son and the Holy Spirit"

(Dr. Barry Johnson, Dr. Anthony King and Dr. Mike Tyler all three doctors say together)

"Amen"

(Doris is in the car with Dr. Robert Stanford who is driving the car, and then Doris asks Dr. Robert Stanford)

"May I ask you where are you taking me?"

"Don't you trust me?"

"More than myself"

"Then from today onwards you do whatever I tell you?'

"Ok"

"That's my baby, from today onwards your worries are my worries?"

"Great?"

(Dr. Robert Stanford stops the car in front of a church, Dr. Robert Stanford gets down from the car then he goes and opens the door for Doris to get down, Doris also gets down from the car, Dr. Robert Stanford then holds Doris' hand and then he says)

"Let's knock on the door of the lord?"

"Yes"

(Dr. Robert Stanford and Doris hand in hand go into the church)

(Inside the church father Joseph is praying in his mind with his eyes closed in front of the statue of Jesus Christ, Dr. Robert Stanford and Doris come there, father Joseph opens his eyes and sees Dr. Robert Stanford and then he says)

"Dr. Robert Stanford! So good to see you?"

(Dr. Robert Stanford bends down and takes the hand of father Joseph and kisses it with his lips and then he says)

"My would be wife Doris and I have come to get the blessings of you and the lord Jesus Christ"

(Doris looks at Dr. Robert Stanford with surprised open eyes, and then she kisses the hand of father Joseph with her lips, and then father Joseph asks Dr. Robert Stanford)

"Would be wife! I don't understand?"

"Father Joseph this is Doris and today we have come to you to become man and wife, Doris is suffering from blood cancer and is going to fight with death starting few hours from now?"

"Oh! But god helps those who help themselves, please bend down"

(Dr. Robert Stanford and Doris bend down in front of father Joseph, father starts praying in his mind, closes his eyes, then father puts his hand on the head of Doris for one minute, and then he puts his hand

on the head of Dr. Robert Stanford for one minute, and then father Joseph says.)

"Now pray in front of lord Jesus Christ"

(Father Joseph moves away and stands beside them, Dr. Robert Stanford and Doris pray in front of the lord Jesus Christ for two minutes, and then Doris tells father Joseph)

"Thank you father Joseph"

"Go my child, the lord is with you"

(Doris kisses the hand of father Joseph then Dr. Robert Stanford kisses the hand of father Joseph, both Dr. Robert Stanford and Doris get up turn and go away, father Joseph turns towards the statue of Jesus Christ and says)

"My lord have pity on this child and fulfill all her wishes"

(Father Joseph does the sign of the Jesus Christ Cross on his chest with his hand and then he says)

"Amen"

(Dr. Robert Stanford is driving his car, Doris is seated beside Dr. Robert Stanford, and then Doris asks Dr. Robert Stanford)

"Can I read your thoughts?"

(Dr. Robert Stanford looks at Doris and then he smiles and asks)

"My thoughts! Can you read them?"

"I can read everything about you?"

"Ok! Go ahead? What is going in my mind?

"You want the clock to go backwards for about five years?"

"Ok! And?"

"You and me starting a life full of happiness, no worry and no tension?"

"Great! Now tell me what do you want as a reward?"

"How much time do we have before we go back to the hospital?"

(Dr. Robert Stanford looks at his watch and then he says)

"Four hours"

"We keep half an hour to go back to hospital, now for three and a half hour I want to live my life fully with you?"

(Dr. Robert Stanford stops his car near a river, and then Robert Stanford and Doris get out of the car, a song in a man's voice starts playing in the background)

"You know how much I love you,

You know how much I care for you"

(Dr. Robert Stanford puts his hand on the shoulder of Doris; Doris puts her hand on the waist of Dr. Robert Stanford, song continues in the man's voice)

"Everyday and night I dreamed of you,

The dreams felt so real"

(Dr. Robert Stanford and Doris goes in to a boat for a ride, the boat is sailing in the water)

"My love yearns for your love,

My body yearns for your body"

(Dr. Robert Stanford takes Doris in his arms)

My lips seeking your lips,

For that burning desire"

(Dr. Robert Stanford kisses Doris on the lips)

"All the nights that I spent alone without you,

The tears in my eyes dried up"

(Doris holds Dr. Robert Stanford tightly; now a song starts in the voice of a woman in the background)

"You are now my love, my life,

My dreams are turning in to reality"

(Doris and Dr. Robert Stanford goes on kissing and holding each other tightly)

"My heart has found true love,

That will never fade again,

My life belongs to you,

My pain, my fear, knows that you are the cure,

In my heart of heart you have taken the place,

By my side you will always be there I know,

You know how much I love you now,

You know how much I care for you now"

(Dr. Robert Stanford and Doris are locked in to each other's arms; a man puts his hand on the shoulder of Dr. Robert Stanford and then he says)

"Sir the boat ride is over?"

"Oh! Come Doris our honeymoon is over"

(Doris gets up and then she tells Dr. Robert Stanford)

"This must be the shortest honeymoon ever?"

"Don't worry, after you get better I'll take you to Atlantic City where we will play games in the casino in the day and play elderly games in the night, ok?

"But we will stay there for at least one month?"

"One month! I'll be drained out in a month?"

"Come on Robert you have to give me at least one child every year?"

"One child every year! How many children do you want?"

"Now our love will last at least ten years, so may be ten children?"

"Ten children! How are going to carry ten children?"

"Two in my hands and two in your hands, two on my shoulders and two on your shoulders, by the time the last six children are born the first four children will start walking on their feet?"

"I think I will be in heaven by that time?"

"No, I will feed you almond and milk everyday?"

(The man on the boat says)

"Would you mind continuing your love story some place else?"

(Dr. Robert Stanford gets angry clenching his fists goes towards the man and then he tells him)

"You lousy bastard, do you know that this lady might not see this boat ever because she has blood cancer?

(Doris holds Dr. Robert Stanford with her hands and the she tells him)

"Please Dr. Robert Stanford this man is just doing his duty?"

(Dr. Robert Stanford eyes fill with tears, and then he tells the man)

"You people don't know how much suffering is there in the world? Everything is ok with you so you don't understand the pain of others?"

(The is ashamed, he looks down and then he says)

"I am sorry I apologize"

(Doris takes Dr. Robert Stanford by grabbing his hand and takes him out of the boat, the man has tears in his eyes, the man on the boat looks up and then he says)

"God please forgive me, as I did not know what I was saying"

(Wisdom the receptionist of Get-Well hospital is lying unconscious on a stretcher and the janitor is taking the stretcher from the corridor, Dr. John Hopes is walking with the stretcher, Dr. Robert Stanford comes there with Doris, seeing Wisdom lying on the stretcher Dr. Robert Stanford asks Dr. John Hopes)

"What happened to wisdom?"

"I can't tell you in front of Doris"

(Doris smiles and then she says)

"I understand, Dr. Robert Stanford I'll go to my room"

"Ok Doris, I'll see you afterwards"

(Doris goes away, Dr. John Hopes laughs and then he tells Dr. Robert Stanford)

"Wisdom fainted looking at the big boobs of a lady"

"What?"

"Let me explain it to you, a lady came and told Wisdom that she has a problem, so wisdom asked what's the problem? The lady said she has a baby-feeding problem and for that which doctor to consult? Wisdom did not understand the meaning of

baby feeding, so Wisdom asked the lady what baby-feeding problem? The lady said that she is not getting enough milk to feed her baby; Wisdom then told her that she should go

to a store to buy milk, the lady said she is not getting enough milk in her boobs, Wisdom asked the lady what boobs? The lady got irritated and lifted her top and seeing such big boobs Wisdom fainted and fell on the floor"

(Dr. Robert Stanford starts laughing and then he tells Dr. John Hopes)

"I think we better shift wisdom's duty to a maternity ward?"

"No chief, in the maternity ward Wisdom will faint every ten minutes?"

"Then I think we should recruit more people like Wisdom in our hospital?"

"More people like Wisdom! Why?"

"So much tension is always there in this hospital, if we recruit more people like Wisdom, every hour we will have a comedy incident and we will forget our tensions"

(Dr John Hopes and Dr. Robert Stanford laughs their guts out, and then Dr. John Hopes tells Dr. Robert Stanford)

"And we can open a new ward called laughing ward?"

"Special ward for the patients who have forgotten how to laugh?"

(Again they laugh and then they both start walking)

(Dr. Mike Tyler, Dr. Barry Johnson, Dr. Anthony King, nurse Jane, nurse Martha, nurse Rosalie and nurse Helen are sitting in the canteen of the hospital having tea, coffee and biscuits. Dr. John Hopes and Dr. Robert Stanford come there, and then Dr. Robert Stanford asks)

"Did you all heard about wisdom fainting?"

(Dr. Mike Tyler laughs and then he says)

"Yes, we all heard it about it? But still we can't believe that Wisdom is such and innocent guy?"

(Dr. Barry Johnson laughs and then he says)

"First time in the history a man faints looking at the best part of a woman's body?"

(Everyone laughs, and then Dr. John Hopes says to Bob who is sitting at the counter of the canteen)

"Bob two coffees please"

(Bob does not answer and starts making coffee, and then Dr. John Hopes asks)

"What's up with Bob?"

(Helen says)

"We all are so busy thinking about our love life, that we have forgotten about Bob's love life?"

(Dr. Robert Stanford asks)

"What's wrong with Bob's love life?"

(Jane says)

"He loves a widow name Madeleine, but the in laws of Madeleine has literally imprisoned Madeleine in their house"

(Bob comes with two coffee mugs, and then he puts the mugs on the table, and then Dr. Robert Stanford says)

"Bob, do you really want to get married to Madeleine?"

"Yes chief, but the in- laws of Madeleine are not letting me even meet her?"

"How do you want to get married?"

"I have the court papers ready with me, the papers just need the sign of Madeleine?"

"Ok, fine, we will all help you to get Madeleine's sign on the court papers"

"But Madeleine's in- laws have a licensed gun with them?"

"Oh! Do any of you have a suggestion?"

(Dr. mike Tyler says)

"We can use some trick and get in to the house?"

(Dr. Barry Johnson says)

"Yes saying that we are checking for a new flu?"

(Dr. Anthony King says)

"To hide our faces we can use the doctor's mask on our face?"

(Dr. Robert Stanford says)

"Ok? In an hour Bob you will be a married man?"

(Bob is happy, he claps his hands and then he says)

"Great! Just like in films?"

(Dr. Robert Stanford smiles and then he says)

"An actor can't be a doctor? But a doctor can be an actor? I have said a great thing about me? Please clap for me?"

(Everybody laughs and then starts clapping)

(Thomas and his wife are having dinner, and then Thomas asks his wife)

"Kate, have you given Madeleine dinner?"

"First let us finish dinner, then whatever is left I will give it to Madeleine"

"Nice, very nice, but it is a good thing that she obeys you and does all the cooking?"

"I have told Madeline that if she does not obey me then I will burn her face"

"Yes, you should sometimes burn her a little so that she remains terrified of you?"

"I never thought of that! I will try and burn her finger?"

"Do that"

(The doorbell rings, and then Thomas says)

"Who must be there at this hour?"

"The next-door bitch must have come to gossip about her daughter in-law? If she is there then tell her to come in the morning?"

"Ok"

(Thomas gets up and goes towards the door and opens it, outside the door Dr. Robert Stanford, Dr. John Hopes, Dr. Barry Johnson, Dr. Anthony King, Dr. Mike Tyler, nurse Helen, nurse Jane, nurse Martha, nurse Rosalie are standing wearing a mask on their faces and doctor's bag in their hands, and then Thomas asks them)

"Who the hell are you all?"

(Dr. Robert Stanford says)

"I am Dr. Eveready and they are my juniors from the hospital"

(Thomas asks)

"Doctors! For what?"

(Dr. Robert Stanford says)

"There is a bribe flu spreading through New York that has struck many people"

"Oh my god! Please come in?"

(They all come into the house, and then Thomas closes the door)

(Dr. Robert Stanford asks Thomas)

"You don't watch news channel?"

"We don't have a television"

(Dr. Robert Stanford looks here and there and then he says)

"We have to check everybody in this house for the bribe flu"

(Kate gets up and then she asks Dr. Robert Stanford)

"Bribe flu! Why is the name bribe flu given to this flu?"

"Because it bribes the flu in the person's body to go in to another person's body"

"Oh! That's dreadful?"

"Doctors, please carry on with your duty?"

"Ok"

(Dr. Robert Stanford tells the other doctors and nurses)

"Please start the operation"

(Dr. Anthony King and nurse Rosalie catch hold of Thomas and make him lie down on the ground and starts checking him with the stethoscope. Dr. Anthony King starts checking Thomas from head and move down towards his stomach. Dr. Barry Johnson and nurse Martha make Kate lie down on the ground and start checking her from her head and move down towards her stomach with the stethoscope, Dr. Robert Stanford moves round and round and then he says)

"I can feel the vibrations of the bribe flu?"

(Dr. Anthony King says)

"Doctor Eveready, the man is clear"

(Then Dr. Barry Johnson says)

"Dr.   Eveready,   the   woman   is   also   clear"

Dr. Robert Stanford—That's again a relief.

(Dr. Robert Stanford with his stethoscope checks the air in the house and then he says)

"But I can still feel the vibrations of the bribe flu in the house?"

(Thomas asks Dr. Robert Stanford)

"Doctor you mean to say that the bribe flu is there in our house?"

"I am a hundred percent sure"

(Then Thomas wife Kate says to her husband)

"Thomas we better let them to check Madeleine"

(Dr. Robert Stanford asks)

"Madeleine! That's your cat?"

(Thomas says)

"No doctor, Madeleine is our daughter in-law"

"Where is she?"

(Kate says)

"She is in the bedroom"

(Dr. Robert Stanford looks at the bedroom door and then he asks)

"The bedroom door is locked! Is your Daughter in-law crazy or what?"

(Kate says)

"She is unbalanced so we keep her locked in the bedroom"

"I think your daughter in-law has the bribe flu?"

(Kate looks at her husband and then she says)

"Oh shit!"

(Thomas tells Kate)

"Kate give the bedroom lock key to the doctor"

(Kate gives the key of the bedroom to Dr. Robert Stanford. Dr. Robert Stanford takes the key; and then he gives the key to Dr. John Hopes and says)

"You and the others go inside the bedroom of Madeleine and check her for bribe flu"

(Dr. John Hopes takes the key from Dr. Robert Stanford and then he says)

"Ok doctor"

(Dr. John Hopes, nurse Helen, Dr. Mike Tyler and nurse Jane goes towards the bedroom door, Dr. John Hopes opens the door and they all go in and close the door, and then Dr. Robert Stanford tells Thomas and his wife Kate)

"You two go and stand in the corner of the room because this bribe flu is a flying flu, it might fly from your daughter in-law to you two and cover your nose with your hands? Thomas and Kate go in the corner and cover their noses with their hands)

(Inside the bedroom Madeleine is sitting on the chair reading a book, Madeleine is a Caucasian, she is five feet five inches tall, shoulder length brown color straight hair, sweet face, she is wearing a jeans and long sleeve shirt, Dr. John Hopes, nurse Helen, Dr. Mike Tyler and nurse Jane comes in to the bedroom, on seeing them Madeleine is shocked, and then she asks in a chocked voice)

"Oh my god! Who are you?"

(Nurse Helen tells Madeleine)

"Madeleine we are from Get-Well hospital where your lover Bob has a canteen?"

"Oh!"

(Jane smiles and then she tells Madeleine)

"And we have come to take you away from here"

(Madeleine smiles and gets up from the chair and then she says)

"Thank you so much"

(Dr. John Hopes tells Madeleine)

"Madeleine, you have to act like you have flu"

(Madeleine is surprised, and then she asks Dr. John Hopes)

"Flu?"

(Dr. Mike Tyler tells Madeleine)

"Yes, we are making a fool of your in laws to take you away from here and get you married to Bob?"

"Great! What do I have to do?"

(Jane tells Madeleine)

"You have to act like you have a high fever and you are just semi-conscious"

"I was a great actor in my school"

(Dr. John Hopes smiles and then he says)

"Madeleine now you have to show your acting talent? Helen and Jane get to work on Madeleine"

(Helen and Jane make Madeleine's face a little reddish, and then they all carry Madeleine and go out of the bedroom)

(Dr. John Hopes, nurse Helen, Dr. Mike Tyler and nurse Jane comes in to the hall carrying Madeline by her hands and legs. And then Dr. John Hopes tell Dr. Robert Stanford)

"Dr. Eveready you were right, this woman is carrying the bribe flu?"

(Madeleine says)

"I don't want to go anywhere, I want to stay with my in laws?"

(Kate runs towards a corner and then she says)

"Do not bring her near us just take her away"

(They all carry Madeleine and go out of the house, and then Dr. Robert Stanford asks Thomas and Kate)

"Do any one of you want to come with us to the hospital?"

(Kate and Thomas say together)

"No"

"But it will take months before she is ok?"

Kate tells Dr. Robert Stanford)

"As it is she is a load on us? If she dies then you only bury her?"

(Dr. Robert Stanford tells Kate and Thomas)

"Your feelings towards your daughter in law are really unique?"

(Then Dr. Robert Stanford and all others go out of the house, and then Thomas tells his wife)

"Kate, in the nick of time we were saved?"

(Kate tells her husband Thomas)

"Let's forget her and eat our food"

(In the ambulance Dr. Robert Stanford, Dr. John Hopes, Dr. Barry Johnson, Dr. Anthony King, nurse Helen, nurse Jane, nurse Martha, nurse Rosalie, Bob and Madeleine are sitting, a box of sweets, two garlands is there, Bob has the court paper in his Hands, and then Dr. Robert Stanford tells Bob)

"Bob and Madeleine both of you put the garlands in each other's neck?"

(Bob puts the garland in Madeleine's neck; Madeleine puts the Garland in Bob's neck, and then Dr. Robert Stanford then tells Bob and Madeleine)

"Now both of you sign on the court papers"

(Madeleine and Bob sign on the court paper; Dr. Robert Stanford takes out two sweets from the sweet box then feeds the sweets to Madeleine and Bob, and then Dr. Robert Stanford says)

"You two are now man and wife"

(Everybody claps, and then Bob says)

"I thank you all"

(Madeleine tells everyone)

"Thank you and god bless you all"

(Then Bob and Madeleine feed the sweets to all the others and then Dr. John Hopes says)

"This must be the first time in the history that a man and woman are married in an ambulance?"

(Everybody laughs and then Helen says))

"In the morning Bob don't forget to go to the court.

"Yes"

(Jane asks)

"Madeleine how does it feel to be married?"

"It looks like a dream come true?"

(Martha asks)

"And you Bob?"

"I still can't believe I am married?"

(Rosalie smiles and then she tells Bob)

"Don't repeat this to Madeleine after the first baby?"

(Everybody laughs and then Bob says)

"I swear upon god in this birth Madeleine will be my only wife"

(Madeleine asks Bob)

"What about the other births?"

"Ok Madeleine you will be my wife for all the next six births"

(Dr. Mike Tyler asks)

"Are you sure Bob?"

"Yeah I am hundred percent sure"

(Dr. Anthony King asks Bob)

"You are making a promise like that to Madeleine?"

(Bob is confused; and then Dr. John Hopes asks Bob)

"Think again! You have promise Madeleine for seven births?"

(Bob looks at everyone and then he asks)

"Did I say something wrong?"

(Everybody laughs and then Madeleine tells Bob)

"Bob you said everything right, they are just playing with you"

"Oh!"

(Then Dr. Robert Stanford asks)

"Bob do you know what to do on the honeymoon night?"

(Bob says)

"Dr. Robert Stanford you have done so much for me? I'll postpone my honeymoon until Doris gets better?"

(Everybody is surprised, and then Dr. Robert Stanford says)

"That's so nice of you Bob?"

(Bob smiles and then he looks at everyone and says)

"We are all just like a family and we will stay like a family?"

(Dr. Robert Stanford says)

"Family! I love the word family?"

(The ambulance stops near Bob's apartment, from the back door of the ambulance Bob and Madeleine gets down, and then Dr. Robert Stanford says)

"Bob and Madeleine you two are going to start a new life from today? Now go and don't look back?

(Bob and Madeleine goes into the apartment building, Helen and then tells Dr. Robert Stanford)

"Dr. Robert Stanford you have done a good deed by getting Bob and Madeleine married? Now god will repay you and one day you will also spend your honeymoon with Doris? These are blessings from all of us?"

(Dr. Robert Stanford eyes starts filling with tears, and then he says)

"When I have well wishers like you all? Definitely god will listen to the prayers?"

(Bob is sitting on the bed wearing only a short pant; he looks at the bedroom door and then he shouts)

"Madeleine, how much more time are you going to take to brush your teeth?"

(Bob hears the voice of Madeline)

"I'll be in just a minute"

"Wait a minute! She has been telling me this for the last ten minutes? I hope she has not changed her mind about me?"

(Bob gets up and walks in the bedroom from right to left and from left to right, Madeline comes there wearing only a short nightdress, and then Bob looks at her and asks)

"What the hell are you wearing?"

"A nightdress?"

"I want you fully dressed up?"

"Fully dressed up! Are you sure?"

"I am the man of the house so I know what I am saying?"

"Ok! I read your message loud and clear?"

(Madeleine goes towards the cupboard and then she opens it and takes out a pant, a shirt and a jacket, then Madeleine takes out her nightdress, she wears the pant, the shirt and the jacket, and then she says)

"May I ask you why you made me a city girl from a jungle Jane?"

(Bob gets back and stands on the bed and then he says)

"Come on the bed and I will make you understand everything?"

(Madeleine climbs on the bed, and then Bob says)

"Now stand up on the bed like me?"

(Madeleine stands up on the bed; Bob takes Madeleine in his arms and kisses her on her head, face, and then lips and after a few seconds Bob starts taking off her clothes, first the shirt, then the pant and finally the jacket. Bob then moves his hands on the body of Madeleine for two minutes, and then Bob says)

"You can again wear the jacket, pant, and the shirt"

"Is it something you saw in a movie or what?"

"My dear wife, I have promised Dr. Robert Stanford that I will do the honeymoon only after Doris gets well? So we have to restrict us? Do you get it?

"You are really sweet Bob, I love you"

(Madeleine comes towards Bob, Bob puts his hand forward and then he says)

"You can make love to me only after you wear your clothes?"

(Madeleine starts laughing and then she asks)

"We go on doing this again and again for how many hours?"

"Until I am tired or you are tired?"

(Madeleine starts wearing the clothes)

(In the Get-Well hospital canteen in the morning Dr. Robert Stanford is standing with his son Robert, Dr. John Hopes is standing with his hand on Helen's shoulder, Dr. Mike Tyler is standing with Jane and they are holding each other, Dr. Barry Johnson is holding hands with Martha, Dr. Anthony King is standing with Rosalie his hand on her waist, opposite them Bob and Madeleine are standing, everybody has a mug in their hands, and then Dr. Robert Stanford says)

"A toast of tea and coffee to the married couple Bob and Madeleine, may they live happily ever after with only minor fights between themselves?"

(Everybody laughs and then they raise their mugs and say)

"Hip, hip, hooray, hip, hip, hooray"

(Everybody drinks his or her tea or coffee from the mug, and then Bob asks)

"Can I say something?"

"Yes you can say as much as you can today because from tomorrow Madeleine will say and you will have to listen to her?"

(Bob says)

"I am a self made man? And the man is the boss of the house? But love is always there in each and every corner of the house?"

(Every man there claps, and then Helen tells Madeleine)

"Madeleine give a fit reply to Bob? All the women are with you?"

(Madeleine smiles and then she says)

"Bob says you can find love in every corner of your house, as I have found out that the corner of the house is full of ants?"

(All the women clap, and then Bob says)

"Madeleine I think you must have moved in circles, my true love is still lying in the corner of the house?"

(Madeleine looks Bob in the eye and then she says)

"I will love you the way you want, I will live the way you want, I will produce babies the way you want, as much baby production as you want, afterwards don't ask me where love has gone?"

(The woman's again clap, and then Bob says)

"God made you love me because I am the best, god made me pick you because you are the best?"

(The man claps, Madeleine tells Bob)

"Heart meets heart and that produces love? There is no man in the world that can make a deal between hearts?"

(Madeleine and Bob kiss each other on the lips, and then Dr. Mike Tyler says)

"I think now they don't need our company, so let's go"

(Helen says)

"As they say love always wins?"

(Dr. John Hopes asks Helen)

"Are you trying to tell me?"

(Helen makes a face at dr. John Hopes and then she tells him)

"No, I was trying to tell myself?"

(Everyone laughs, and then Bob tells Madeleine))

"Madeleine, your lips are so sensational that they give an electric shock to my body?"

"When you hug me so tightly, my heart begins to flutter"

"I give my love to you, you give your love to me?"

"I wish this moment to come to a stand still, I wish the clock could stop and the time remains stand still?"

(Bob kisses Madeleine on the lips, everyone looks at each other and then they smile and go away from the canteen, and then Bob picks Madeleine in his arms and says)

"I love you, I love you"

(Bob moves round and round with Madeleine in his arms)

(Helen is looking at the work sheet of the hospital, Rosalie comes running and then she tells Helen)

"Helen, Jane's mother has been brought to the hospital, she seems in very bad shape?"

(Helen leaves the work sheet on the table and then she says)

"Oh my god!"

(Helen and Rosalie start running through the corridor of the hospital, and then Helen asks Rosalie)

"What's wrong with her?"

"She is in a trance"

"Trance! What do you mean?"

"Like something has blocked her brain"

(Inside the hospital room Jane's mother is lying on the bed, her eyes steady in one-position, Jane's aunty and uncle are there, Dr. John Hopes and Dr. Barry Johnson are checking Jane's mother, Jane is crying, and then she asks)

"What has happened to my mother? My aunty says she has not eaten anything for a day? Please help my mother?"

"Jane please, let me and Dr. Barry Johnson check her first?"

(Dr. Barry Johnson tells Jane)

"Jane at your mother's age sometimes a person loses their will to live? So that's why they don't feel like eating anything?"

(Helen and Rosalie come inside the room and they look at Jane's mother lying on the bed, and then Jane says)

"Mother? Mother? Say something?"

(Helen goes and takes Jane in her arms and then she says)

"Jane please control yourself? Mother will be just fine?"

(Jane starts crying, and then Dr. Barry Johnson says)

"Dr. John Hopes there seems to be nothing wrong with her?"

"Yes Dr. Barry Johnson, let us put her on glucose?"

"Yes"

(Then Dr. John Hopes tells Jane)

"Jane, don't worry? Your mother will come out of her trance?

(Jane asks)

"But how Dr. John Hopes?"

"Like remind her of what she loved doing the most and her mind will become normal, these kind of cases can be cured very quickly if the patient finds something important that she loved to do?"

(Helen asks)

"Dr. John Hopes you mean that she has to be taken in the past?"

"Correct, like what she loved to do? But as the time pass she might go deeper in to her trance? So whatever has to be done should be done soon?"

(Helen takes Jane out of the room, and then Dr. Barry Johnson tells Dr. John Hopes)

"We have to run some tests on Carol?"

"Yes, we have to; Jane was so upset that I did not want her to upset her more, but this case does not seem that easy?"

(Jane's aunty asks)

"Doctor, is it serious?"

(Dr. John Hopes says)

"No, No, what I was trying to say that the patient could remain like that for years to come, but to get the patient out of the trance you need to help the patient's blockage in the head completely washed away?"

(Jane's aunty starts crying, and then Jane's uncle takes her wife out of the room)

(Jane, Helen, Martha, Rosalie, Dr. Mike Tyler, Bob and Madeleine is in the hospital canteen, and then Dr. Mike Tyler tells Jane)

"Jane your mother will be fine soon? Only thing she has to be taken out of her trance?"

"How?"

"To all four of you she is a mother, right?"

"Right?

"Think about something that Jane's mother loved the most?"

(Helen asks Dr. mike Tyler)

"Dr. you mean to say that Jane's mother will get out of the trance if make her mind alert?"

"Yes Helen? It has to be something that will reach her brain and she reacts?

"So playing with her brain will only get her out of her trance? And medicine?

"Medicine will only give her mind rest, to get her out of the trance you have to play with her brain, only one such incident will bring her out of the trance?"

(Jane starts crying, Dr. Mike Tyler takes Jane in his arms, Helen looks at Martha and

Rosalie telling them by her eyes that they should go away. Martha, Rosalie and Helen go out of the canteen, Bob also goes towards his counter, and then Mike Tyler tells Helen)

"Jane take it easy, look you have to be very strong, this is the time you have to control your feelings and think only of getting your mother back to normal"

"This is so sudden Mike? I never thought that this problem would arise in my life?"

"I am with you? Everybody else is with you? If you become normal then only the others can think of a way to get your mother out of her trance?"

(Jane wipes her tears and then she says)

"You are right Mike, I promise no more tears will come in my eyes?"

"That's my baby"

(Helen is alone sitting opposite the reception counter, she is lost in her thoughts, she gets up and goes towards the counter, and then Wisdom tells Helen)

"Helen to get Jane's mother out of the trance do you want me to help?"

"What can you do?"

"I am a very bad baseball player, if Jane's mother Carol sees me playing baseball she will definitely laugh and she will get out of her trance?"

(Helen looks at wisdom and then she hugs Wisdom and tells him)

"You stupid fool you have given me an idea?"

"Helen either you call me stupid or fool?

"Please Wisdom now don't disturb me?"

(Helen picks up the phone receiver and then she dials a number, she waits and then she says)

"Dr. Jill Scott I am Helen speaking from the Get-Well hospital, I want your help? Will you please come with your boyfriend Dr. Liver bones to Get-Well hospital? Yes it is very important? Ok? Thank you"

(Helen puts the receiver down on the phone and then she goes running, and then Wisdom says)

"She called me stupid and a fool? And then she said that I had given her an idea?

(Dr. Mike Tyler and Jane are sitting in the canteen having tea, Rosalie comes there running and then she tells Jane)

"Jane come quick, Helen is trying to do a miracle?"

"Miracle! What miracle?"

"Don't ask me anything as there is no time? We have to run?"

(Jane, Dr. Mike Tyler and Rosalie goes running out of the canteen, and then Bob Tells Madeleine)

"This miracle I don't want to miss? I think I should take some chocolate donuts with me?"

"Get the donuts fast Bob?"

"Ok"

(Helen, Dr. John Hopes, Dr. Liver Bones and Dr. Jill Scott are playing pool, Helen and Dr. John Hopes are in one team, Dr. Liver Bones and Dr. Jill Scott are in the other team, doctors and nurses are watching the pool game, Martha brings Jane's mother Carol on the wheel chair and stops near the pool table, Dr. John Hopes sees Jane's mother Carol and then he tells Helen)

"Now please don't miss this easy shot Helen? The solid ball should go in the pocket?"

(Helen with the stick pushes the white ball towards the solid ball, the sound of the white ball hitting the solid ball echoes through the room, Carol hears the sound and looks at the pool table, and then Dr. John Hopes tells Helen)

"Helen you again missed the shot? If you play like this we will lose the game?"

(Dr. Jill Scott says)

"Dr. John hopes you better change your partner Helen with some other partner or you will lose the game and the respect of your hospital?"

(Dr. John Hopes says)

"Nobody plays better then Helen? So I am stuck with her?"

(Dr. Liver Bones tells Dr. John Hopes and Helen)

(Next time first practice and then challenge us for the pool game?"

(Dr. Jill Scott hits the color ball with the white ball; the color ball goes in to the pocket, and then Dr. liver Bones claps and says)

"What a great shot Dr. Jill Scott"

"Thank you Dr. Liver Bones"

(Jane, Dr. Mike Tyler and Rosalie come there, Dr. Jill Scott puts two more colored balls into the pocket, and then she misses a shot. Dr. John Hopes takes the strike, Dr. John Hopes puts two solid balls into the pocket, then Dr. John Hopes misses the shot, Dr. Liver Bones takes the strike and puts two colored balls in to the pocket, then Dr. Liver Bones misses a shot, Helen gets ready to strike the solid ball with the white ball, and then she says)

"This is a very difficult shot Dr. John Hopes?"

"I can see that Helen? But you have to make this impossible shot possible?"

(Dr. Liver Bones says)

"Helen if you take this shot then we will accept that we have lost the game? Otherwise you two have to accept that you have lost the game?"

(The shot is a difficult one; the white ball has to put the black ball in to the pocket as well as put the last solid ball in to the pocket, and then Dr. Jill Scott says)

"Helen and Dr. John Hopes accept defeat and you will at least save your self-respect?"

(Dr. Liver Bones looks at everyone and then he says)

"If anybody in this room takes this shot then I and Dr. Jill Scot swear that we will never play pool again, but if Helen does not take the shot then we will take away this pool table with us?"

(Helen is ready to strike the ball, and then Carol says)

"Please stop Helen?"

(Everybody is surprised at hearing the voice of Carol, Carol slowly gets up from the wheel chair, then Carol slowly goes towards the pool table and takes the stick from Helen, Carol looks at the black ball then the solid ball, Carol moves her eyes through the pockets, Carol hits the white ball with the stick, the white ball goes and hits the black ball, the black ball goes in to the right hand opposite pocket, the white ball then bounces from the table and hits the solid ball, the solid ball goes in to the left hand side middle pocket, everybody is shocked at this shot, Carol looks at everybody smiling, Jane comes running towards her mother Carol and then she says)

"Mother!"

"Jane, did you see this shot?"

"Yes mother, what a shot"

(Jane hugs her mother, everybody claps, and then Bob comes with a tray of chocolate donuts and then he tells Carol)

"Never seen a shot like this in my life carol?"

(Carol looks at the chocolate donuts and then she asks Bob)

"Can I take one chocolate donut?"

"This full tray of chocolate donuts is for you mother"

(Carol takes the tray from Bob's hand and starts eating the donuts, Helen goes towards Dr. Jill Scott and Dr. Liver Bones and then she says)

"Thank you Dr. Jill Scott and Dr. Liver Bones, I appreciate it"

(Dr. Jill Scott hugs Helen and then she says)

"Helen, you are fantastic"

(Dr. Liver Bones puts his hand on the side of his head and then he tells Helen)

"You made the impossible possible, I salute you"

(Dr. Liver Bones salutes Helen, Helen says)

"It is just that god has been kind to me"

(Dr. Jill Scott and Dr. Liver Bones go away, Jane comes running and hugs Helen and then she says)

"How can I ever thank you enough?"

"You have told me no thank you and no sorry between friends?"

(Jane kisses Helen on both the cheeks, and then she says))

"God bless you Helen"

(Helen, Jane, Martha, Rosalie, Jane's mother Carol, Dr. John Hopes, Dr. Mike Tyler, Dr. Anthony King, Dr. Barry Johnson, Jane's aunty and Jane's uncle are sitting in a restaurant having drinks and dinner, and then Carol says)

"Thanks to Helen I got a new lease of life"

(Helen smiles and then she hugs Carol and says)

"Anything for a mother"

(Jane tells Carol)

"Mother now I am going to stay with you?"

(Carol asks Jane)

"That means you will leave your job?"

(Jane says)

"If I have to I will leave my job mother? You are more important to me?"

(Dr. Mike Tyler asks Jane)

"What about me?"

(Jane asks Dr. Mike Tyler)

"What do you mean by that?"

(Dr. Mike Tyler asks Jane)

"I mean to tell you that do I have to stay at your house after marriage?"

(Everyone laughs; Carol pats the face of Dr. Mike Tyler and then she tells him)

"My future son in-law, you don't want to be a hand peck husband, do you?"

(Dr. Mike Tyler smiles and then he says)

"I don't mind because I love Jane and as they say everything is fair in love and war?"

(Jane Tells Dr. Mike Tyler)

"Everything depends on my mother?"

(Carol asks Jane)

"Everything! What?"

(Jane tells her Mother Carol)

"Like I come and live with you in New Jersey or you come and live with me in New York?"

(Carol asks Jane)

"And after you marry?"

(Jane looks at Dr. Mike Tyler, he smiles and then he tells Carol)

"My future mother in law, definitely you will stay with Jane and me?"

(Carol says)

"I think I also need a change and my sister and her husband can take care of my house and the candle business in New Jersey?"

(Carol's sister tells Carol)

"Sister you have taken a wise decision, on weekends you can come and visit us or we can come and visit you here?"

(Carol says)

"It is ok with me"

(Helen says)

"I think I will have to buy three new dresses?"

(Everyone looks at Helen surprised, and then Martha asks Helen)

"Three new dresses! Why?"

(Helen smiles and then she says)

"Martha you and Rosalie want to come for Jane's wedding with out clothes?"

(Everyone laughs, and then Rosalie says)

"Martha and me would not mind coming without clothes but Dr. Anthony King and Dr. Barry Johnson would feel embarrassed?"

(Dr. Anthony King says)

"Rosalie I love you and not your clothes?"

(Everyone laughs, and then Dr. Barry Johnson says)

"I also would not mind Martha without clothes, because I like her face and not the body?"

(Everyone again laughs, and then Dr. John Hopes asks)

"What about Helen and me?"

(Jane says)

"Dr. John Hopes Helen just said that she is going to buy three dresses? You can have one of them?"

(Everyone laughs, and then Dr. John Hopes says)

"I don't mind? But I won't put on lipstick?"

(Everyone laughs, and then Carol looks up and says)

"I pray to god that the friendship you all share remains forever"

(Jane's uncle says)

"Let's have one more drink to Carol's wish?"

(Dr. John Hopes says)

"Sure?"

(Dr. John Hopes calls the waiter, the waiter comes and then Dr. John Hopes says))

"Brother one more drink for everyone"

(Waiter says)

"Yes sir"

(Waiter goes away, and then Carol asks)

"Helen, Martha, and Rosalie, what are your plans for the future?"

(Helen says)

"Dr. John Hopes and I have given each other one-year, if everything is fine after one year, we marry"

(Martha says)

"Dr. Barry Johnson's father had borrowed money from people, now he has to pay up so our marriage will have to wait"

(Rosalie says)

"Dr. Anthony King has four sisters who are still to get married; after they marry we will marry"

(Carol says)

"Oh! Leave it to god? He will decide what is good for you three?"

(Jane makes a Jesus Christ Cross sign on her chest and then she says)

"Amen to that"

(Dr. Robert Stanford is in his cabin, the intercom phone bell Rings, Dr. Robert Stanford picks up the receiver and then he say)

"Chief"

(Then Robert Stanford listens to the voice of the other side and then he says)

"I'll be there in a minute"

(Dr. Robert Stanford puts the receiver down, and then he takes out his mobile from his pocket and then he dials a number)

(Dr. John Hopes who is in restaurant having dinner with the Dr. Barry Johnson, Dr. Anthony King, Dr. Mike Tyler, Helen, Jane, Martha, Rosalie, Carol, Carol's sister and her husband hears his mobile ringing, he takes out the mobile phone from his pocket and then he looks at the number on the mobile phone and puts the mobile on his ear and then he says)

"Yes chief?"

(Dr. Robert Stanford says on his mobile)

"Dr. John Hopes there is an emergency, the film actress Joan Banks has been hurt in an accident and she has been brought to our hospital, can you please come as soon as possible and get Dr. Barry Johnson with you?"

(Dr. John Hopes says on his Mobile)

"Right chief, Dr. Barry Johnson and I will be there as fast as we can?"

(Dr. Robert Stanford says on his mobile)

"Thank you Dr. John Hopes"

(Dr. John Hopes switches off his mobile phone and then he says)

"Sorry but Dr. Barry Johnson and I have to go? There is an emergency at the hospital?

(Carol says)

"No problem John, work is worship"

"Ok everybody bye, let's go Dr. Barry Johnson?"

(Dr. Barry Johnson says)

"Bye"

(Dr. John Hopes and Dr. Barry Johnson get up and go away, and then Carol says)

"Jane what are your plans for your wedding?"

"Let me say this Sunday?"

(Everybody is surprised at Jane's decision, and then Helen asks)

"This Sunday! Are you sure?"

(Jane smiles and asks)

"Is it to late? Make it before Sunday?"

(Helen tells Jane)

"No, no, what I want to say is so many preparations are to be made?"

(Jane tells Helen, Martha and Rosalie)

"You are my friends? So it is your look out to get everything ready by Sunday?"

(Martha says)

"Ok Jane"

(Rosalie says)

"I will dress up like a bride, because I never know when I will marry?"

(Dr. Anthony King says)

"Don't worry Rosalie I will get all my four sisters married at one time?"

(Everyone laughs, and then Dr. Mike Tyler says)

"I am going on leave from tomorrow? God has been really kind to me"

(Carol says)

"Dr. Mike Tyler you should thank me?"

(Dr. Mike Tyler gets up and lifts Carol in his arms and then he dances and says)

"Thank you future mother in-law, thank you my future mother in-law"

(Tora Banks is sitting on the bench in the hospital corridor. Tora Banks is an African American; she is five feet nine inches tall, shoulder length hair, black eyes, a very nice figure, and a beautiful face, she is wearing a black backless top, and a short black skirt, Dr. John Hopes and Dr. Barry Johnson come there in their formal clothes, they both stare at Tora Banks, and she asks them)

"Excuse me?"

(Dr. Barry Johnson says)

"Ma'am, we are the doctors who are going to operate on your daughter Joan Banks"

"Oh!"

(Tora Banks extends her hand, Dr. Barry Johnson shakes hand with Tora Banks and goes on looking at her face, and then Tora Banks asks)

"Doctor, I think that the hand shaking is over, do you mind leaving my hand?"

(Dr. Barry Johnson says)

"Yes ma'am"

(Dr. Barry Johnson leaves the hand of tora banks, and then Tora Banks asks Dr. John Hopes)

"Doctor do you also want to shake hands with me?"

"No ma'am"

(Tora Banks asks)

"Well?"

(Dr. John Hopes says)

"Ma'am may I ask you how the knife got stuck inside the stomach of your daughter Joan?

(Tora Banks says)

"Today she wanted to prepare dinner for me, she was cutting vegetables, she fell down and the knife she had in her hand scratched her stomach, I have already given the statement to the police?"

(Dr. John Hopes looks at Dr. Barry Johnson surprised, and then tells Tora Banks)

"Oh!"

(Tora Banks says)

"Now will you please go and see my daughter?"

(Dr. John Hopes says)

"Ok"

(Tora Banks says)

"I am going to have a cup of coffee? This is my card and after you examine her give me a call?"

(Tora Banks gives a card to Dr. John Hopes; Dr. John Hopes takes the card and then he says)

"Ok ma'am, I'll call you?"

(Tora Banks just walks away, and then Dr. Barry Johnson tells Dr. John Hopes)

"What a beautiful lady, when the mother is so beautiful, how beautiful her daughter will be?"

(Dr. John Hopes smiles and then he says)

"I think her daughter will be a bombshell, let's check her out?"

(Dr. John Hopes and Dr. Barry Johnson go into the room)

(In the room Joan Banks is lying on the bed of the hospital, Joan Banks is African American, she is five foot eight inches tall, long black wavy hair, brown eyes, perfect figure, beautiful face, she is wearing a knee length white dress. Dr. Barry Johnson and Dr. John Hopes comes inside the room, and then Dr. John Hopes looks at Joan Banks and says)

"Hello Joan Banks, I am Dr. John Hopes and this is Dr. Barry Johnson"

(Joan Banks says)

(Joan Banks says)

"Hello"

(Dr. John Hopes says)

"We want to examine the wound?"

(Joan Banks says)

"Go ahead"

(Dr. John Hopes removes the cloth from the wound, Dr. Barry Johnson goes on looking at the face of Joan Banks, and then Dr. John Hopes tells Joan Banks)

"The wound is deep so we will have to stitch it up?"

(Joan Banks asks)

"Oh! How many days I have to stay in the hospital?"

(Dr. Joan hopes says)

"About a week"

(Joan Banks says)

"About a week! No doctor I have a shooting day after tomorrow?"

"You better cancel your shooting"

(Joan Banks says)

"What do you mean cancel my shooting? My Film is at the final stage?"

(Dr. John Hopes smiles and then he says)

"Sorry ma'am there is no other option?

(Joan Banks sits up on the bed and then she says angrily)

"You are a doctor and you don't have any other options? I have to leave the hospital by tomorrow! Is that clear?"

(Dr. John Hopes gets angry and then he says)

"Ma'am we are doctors and not your servants that you can order us around? If you think that we are not capable then you better go to another hospital and remember that this is a hospital and not your shooting set, ok?

(Dr. John Hopes burst of anger surprises Joan Banks, and then she says in a soft voice)

"I am sorry doctor, I apologize"

(Dr. John Hopes says)

"That's ok"

(Then Joan Banks smiles and then she says)

"Doctor at least you could have smiled and said that's ok?"

(Dr. John Hopes extends his hand, and then he smiles and says)

"I am also sorry?"

(Joan Banks shakes hand with Dr. John Hopes and then she says)

"What a good actor! You should be in the movies?"

(Everyone laughs, Joan Banks kisses the hand of Dr. John Hopes and then she says)

"Now your hand won't shake while putting stitches on my stomach?"

(Everyone again laughs)

(Tora Banks is moving from left to right and from right to left outside the operation theatre, Tora Bank's husband Fred Banks comes there, Fred Banks is Caucasian, six feet one inches tall, has brown shoulder length hair, sea green eyes, he looks like a Greek God, he is very handsome, he is wearing light blue colored track pants, and a light blue colored polo t-shirt, and then Fred Banks asks Tora Banks)

"How is Joan?"

(Tora Banks says angrily)

"Am I god or what that I am able to know that what is going on in the operation theatre?"

"You don't have to be rude Tora?"

"Would you mind leaving me alone?"

"Day by day you are getting worse?"

"So please stop talking to me?"

"It is my fault that I had always ignored your shortcomings?"

"Why don't you ignore me all together?"

"Just shut up"

"You shut up"

(Dr. John Hopes comes out of the operation theatre, on seeing him Tora Banks asks him)

"Doctor how is Joan?"

"I have put stitches on her stomach, she is fine but right now she is unconscious"

(Tora banks asks)

"Can I take her home after she regains consciousness?"

(Dr. John Hopes says)

"Ma'am the wound will take at least one week to heal, after that she has to take rest for at least one month?"

"Day after tomorrow she has her shooting? She has to be on the shooting set?"

"I can't give her permission to leave the hospital for one week"

"Who are you to decide that?"

"Ma'am, I am a doctor?"

"Does not make any difference to me?"

"Joan remains in the hospital for one week? Is that clear?

"You can't stop me from taking Joan home today?"

"Yes I can, in her sub consciousness Joan was saying mom don't make me angry otherwise I'll hurt myself, I can always give this statement to the police or the press?"

(Joan bank's Father Fred Banks comes there, and then he tells Dr. John Hopes)

"No doctor you can keep Joan in the hospital for a week, by the way I am Joan's father, Fred Banks"

(Fred Banks extends his hand, Dr. John Hopes shakes Fred Banks Hand and then he says)

"Hello sir, I am Dr. John Hopes"

"Glad to meet you Doctor"

"Me too, ok I have to go?"

"See you doctor"

(Dr. John Hopes looks at Tora Banks then turns and goes away, and then Tora banks asks her husband)

"Who are you to take a decision about Joan?"

"I think you have forgotten that I am her father?"

"Yeah I always forget! Why don't you Divorce me?"

"Ok I will go to the court and I will tell the court for your misdeeds to our daughter and I'll see that I get custody of Joan from the court"

"Joan is an adult and the court will ask Joan's decision whom she wants to stay with?"

"Joan would rather stay alone then stay with you? Joan is only with us because we are together, the day we separate Joan will walk away from our lives"

"You son of a bitch?

"You know the real meaning of bitch because you are one"

"Why don't you get out of my sight?"

"If you had not been Joan's mother I would not even spit on you"

"This is a hospital otherwise I would have scratched your face off"

"Don't even try it Tora otherwise you will regret that all your life"

"Once Joan gets better I am going to severe all ties with you, I'll also see that you never even meet Joan"

"You have made my life hell, now I'll see that everyday of your life will be worse than hell, your kind of woman rots only in hell"

(Tora Banks goes away angrily, Fred Banks looks at her then goes and sits down on the bench)

(Jane and Dr. Mike Tyler are walking on the road, and then Dr. Mike Tyler says)

"Jane it was not nice to say we want to be alone and walk away from the restaurant?"

"They will understand? Only few days are remaining for our marriage?"

(Dr. Mike Tyler takes Jane in her arms then kisses her on her lips and then asks her)

"Anything important you want to talk about us?"

"Yes"

"What?"

"Are you sure you will be comfortable living with my mother in your house?"

"Yeah I am sure"

"Look I want our marriage to be successful"

"Ok, ask me what more do you want to ask? But you don't mind if I go on kissing you?

"From today onwards I am your property, you can kiss me, and you can squeeze me, now tell me if suppose my mother wants to go again to her house in New Jersey after we marry I will definitely go with her, then what?"

"We both will go and live with her in New Jersey"

"You like me so much?"

"No"

"You like to be with me?"

"No"

"If I break this marriage you will cry?"

"No"

"What does that mean?"

"Look you asked me I like you more then myself? You said I like to be with you? I love to be with you? You said that I would cry if you break this marriage? I would rather love to die than cry if you break the marriage?"

"So you were playing with me? Now I will show you the real Jane?"

(Jane starts making love to Dr. Mike Tyler, Dr. Mike Tyler lifts Jane in his arms and starts walking, and then Jane goes on kissing and hugging Dr. Mike Tyler)

(Dr. John Hopes is at the hospital reception counter, he is making entries in the chart sheet of Joan Banks, receptionist Kai who is sitting behind the reception counter asks Dr. John Hopes)

"Doctor can I get you a coffee?"

"Yeah please kai?"

(Kai goes away, Dr. John Hopes looks at his watch and then he says)

"It is eleven thirty in the night?

(Dr. Barry Johnson comes towards the reception counter, and then Dr. John Hopes asks him)

"Barry is Joan ok?"

"Yes John, she will regain consciousness in a few minutes"

"Ok, but we will have to wait until she regains consciousness?"

"Yeah we will have to? But John Joan is more beautiful then her
  mother?"

"You are right? But Joan's father is also a handsome guy?"

"You met him?"

"Yeah I met him, but Joan's mother is a real Bitch?"

"Why? What happened?

"She even tried to act smart with me?"

"Did you give it to her or not?"

"Yeah, I insulted her"

"I think that the sooner Joan is discharged from the hospital the
  better for us?

*(The receptionist Kai comes with a coffee mug and gives it to Dr.
John Hopes, and then Dr. John Hopes tells her)*

"Thank you kai?"

"My pleasure, Dr. Barry Johnson can I get you a coffee also?

"No, thank you"

*(Kai goes towards the reception counter and sits down, and then Dr.
John Hopes tells her)*

"Dr. Barry Johnson let's go? Kai if there is any call for me I'll be in
  my cabin?"

"Ok"

*(Dr. John Hopes and Dr. Barry Johnson are walking in the hospital
corridor, Dr. John Hopes is having sips of coffee from the mug he
has in his hand, and Dr. John Hopes tells Dr. Barry Johnson)*

"Jane and Dr. Mike Tyler will be marrying on Sunday, what have
  you thought about Martha and yourself?"

"I'll let time decide it?"

"You have laid her?"

"No"

"She does not want to get laid?"

"She wants to get laid, but I don't want screw her"

"You don't want to screw her! Why?"

"I have my own reservations"

"Reservations?"

"Yes, I don't want to have sex with Martha before marriage?"

"What is wrong in having sex before marriage?"

"The fun and excitement goes away"

"I don't understand your logic Barry?"

"I have seen it with my own eyes, the couples that had sex before marriage always ends up in divorce?"

"Come on Barry! Grow up?"

"John if Helen let's you have sex with her, will you do it?"

"Yeah sure, I would rather love to have sex before marriage"

"Look John, take my advice that if you want to marry a woman don't have sex with her? Other women are there with whom you can have sex?

"I did not know you were such an old fashioned person? Barry you should have been born in the nineteen fifties?"

(Dr. Barry Johnson laughs and then he says)

"I am what I am? Nobody can change me?"

"Please Barry don't tell anybody what you have told me, they will think that you are a crazy man"

"John marriage is a sacred thing for me? But will you have sex with outside women?"

"Barry you don't eat your home food every day, sometimes you also eat outside food?"

(Nurse Flora comes, and then she tells Dr. John Hopes)

"Dr. John Hopes, ma'am Joan is conscious and wants to see you?"

"Ok, I'll be there in a minute Flora?"

"Ok Doctor"

(Nurse Flora goes away, and then Dr. John Hopes asks Dr. Barry Johnson)

"Barry you want to come?"

"John Joan has asked only for you? Your logic of sometimes eating outside food may come true?"

"I hope my luck changes like you said?"

"As they say, try and try and you may succeed?"

(Dr. John Hopes winks at Dr. Barry Johnson and then he goes away)

(Joan Banks is looking at herself in the small mirror that nurse Flora has in her hands, and then Joan Banks asks Flora)

"How do I look?"

"You look beautiful ma'am"

"Tell me about Dr. John Hopes?"

"He is a very good doctor"

"I want to ask about his nature?"

"He is a simple person and has a heart of gold"

"You know so much about him! Are you in love with him?"

"What are you saying ma'ams?"

"A nurse loving a doctor is not a sin?'

"Dr. John Hopes has a girlfriend named Helen and she is a nurse in this hospital?"

"Oh! Interesting! Does the nurse Helen also love him?"

"I think so"

"Ok, put the mirror on the table nurse, you can wait outside and when Dr. John Hopes comes please wait outside and don't come in with him?"

"Ok"

(Nurse Flora puts the mirror on the table where medicines are kept, and then she goes out of the room, Joan Banks smiles and then she says to herself)

"A nurse and doctor in love! An interesting story for a movie?"

(Outside the room of Joan Banks nurse Flora is standing, Dr. John Hopes comes and then he asks Flora)

"Hey Flora why are you standing outside the room?"

"Ma'am Joan told me to wait outside"

"Wait outside! Strange?"

(Dr. John Hopes opens the door and then he goes inside the room)

(Inside the room Joan Banks is looking towards the door of the room, Dr. John Hopes come inside the room and then he asks Joan Banks)

"Ma'am you wanted to see me, are you ok?"

"I am just fine, I called you because I wanted to talk to you"

"Talk to me! About what?"

"Would you like to marry me?"

(Dr. John Hopes is shocked to hear Joan Banks talk like this, and then he says)

"What?"

"I asked you a simple question? Would you like to marry me?"

"I already have a girlfriend?"

"Does not make any difference to me"

"My girlfriend and me are going to marry in future?

"So what?"

"So what!"

"You have a right to change your mind?"

"I don't think I'll be changing my mind"

"I'll see to it that you do"

"Now if you excuse me?"

"No I don't excuse you"

"If you have any problems tell me? Otherwise I have to go home?"

"My wound is paining"

"I can give you pain killers?"

"No I want you to stay"

"You can call your mother or father to stay with you"

"They have time only to fight with each other and I told them to go home"

"Nurse flora is also there to take care of you?"

"Look doctor if you don't stay with me here, I'll just go home"

"You are black mailing me?"

"You can think anything, I want you to stay here with me"

"Ma'am please, I had a very tiring day, I need a good night sleep, and tomorrow I have an operation to do?"

"Ok, doctor you can go"

(Joan Banks extends her hand, Dr. John Hopes shakes hands with Joan Banks, Joan Banks holds the hand of Dr. John Hopes for a few seconds, Dr. John Hopes feels a vibration inside his body, he takes away his hand from the hand of Joan Banks, and then Joan Banks smiles and says)

"Good night doctor, have a sound sleep"

"Good night"

(Dr. John Hopes turns and goes out of the room, and then Joan Banks says to herself)

"You are going to fall for me hook, line, and sinker"

(A wicked smile comes on the face of Joan Banks)

(Dr. Barry Johnson is in the cabin of Dr. John Hopes, Dr. John Hopes come in to the cabin, and then Dr. Barry Johnson asks him)

"What happened?

"Barry, Joan is a very fast one?"

"What do you mean?"

"She said she wants to get married to me?"

"That means she really is a fast one?"

"Better we get her away from this hospital as soon as possible?"

"John be very careful?"

"Yes Barry? She would spoil my life? The way she held my hand while saying good night, a current passed through my body?"

"These kinds of girls only know how to break hearts?"

"I think something is very wrong with her? From tomorrow you attend to her?"

"Forgets the incident John, let's go home?"

"Yeah, let's go"

(Dr. John Hopes opens his cabin door, and then Dr. John Hopes and Barry Johnson go out of the cabin)

(Jane and Dr. Mike Tyler's wedding is going on in the church, Jane and Dr. Mike Tyler are standing in front of the priest, the priest asks Dr. Mike Tyler)

"Do you take this lady as your wedded wife?"

"Yes I do"

(The priest then asks Jane)

"Do you take this man as your wedded husband?"

"Yes I do"

(And then the priest tells Dr. Mike Tyler)

"You are man and wife, now you can kiss the bride"

(Dr. Mike Tyler kisses Jane on the lips, everyone claps, Helen, Rosalie, Martha, Dr. John Hopes, Dr. Anthony King, Dr. Barry Johnson and Dr. Robert Stanford comes near Jane and Dr. Mike Tyler, and then Dr. Robert Stanford says)

"Congratulations to you Jane and mike"

(Dr. Mike Tyler and Jane say together)

"Thank you chief"

(Dr. Robert Stanford hugs Jane and Dr. Mike Tyler and then Helen, Rosalie and Martha hugs Dr. Mike Tyler and Jane and then all three say)

"Wish you both a happy married life"

(Dr. Mike Tyler and Jane say together)

"Thank you"

(Dr. John Hopes Dr. Anthony King, Dr. Barry Johnson all three hugs Jane and Dr. Mike Tyler and then they say)

"May god bless you with at least eleven children?"

(Everyone laughs, and then Jane says)

"Please then don't have any children of yours? Because we will give at least two of our children to each of you?"

(Everyone laughs; Jane's mother Carol comes with her sister and her husband, then Carol hugs Jane and Dr. Mike Tyler and says)

"May god give you all the happiness you deserve?"

(Dr. Mike Tyler and Jane say together)

"Thank you mother"

(Then Jane's aunty and uncle hug Jane and Dr. Mike Tyler and then they say)

"Congratulations to you both and have a happy life"

(Dr. Mike Tyler and Jane say together)

"Thank you?

(Carol tells everyone)

"Let's go we have to get things done for the reception in the night?"

(Everyone starts going out of the church)

(Nurse flora is giving medicine to Joan Banks, then Flora gives the glass of water to Joan Banks, Joan Banks drinks the water and then she gives the Glass to nurse flora and asks)

"Nurse I have not seen Dr. John hopes today?"

"Ma'am today nurse Jane is getting married to Dr. Mike Tyler"

"Oh! So a nurse has trapped a doctor into getting married to her?"

"Ma'am nurse Jane and Dr. Mike Tyler were going steady for the last six months"

"A nurse marring a Doctor! It only happens in movies? Not in reality?

(Nurse Flora does not say anything, and then Joan Banks tells her)

Nurse you go outside sit? If I need you I'll ring the bell?"

Ok ma'am"

(Nurse Flora goes out of the room, and then Joan Banks smiles and says)

"I will have to extra charming to Dr. John Hopes to trap him into marring me?"

(At the reception in the night, Jane is with Dr. Mike Tyler and beside them are Helen, Dr. John Hopes, Rosalie, Dr. Anthony King, Martha, Dr. Barry Johnson and Dr. Robert Stanford with Doris's son Robert, Dr. Mike Tyler takes Jane in his arms and kisses her on the lips, for two minutes Dr. Mike Tyler goes on kissing Jane on the lips, and then Dr. Robert Stanford tells Dr. Mike Tyler)

"Buddy you have got full night ahead of you?"

(Everyone laughs, and Dr. John hopes tells Dr. Mike Tyler)

"Anyway it was a nice show?"

(Dr. Mike Tyler smiles and then he says)

"John, I wanted to convince Jane that I really love her?"

(Everyone laughs, and then Helen tells Dr. Mike Tyler)

"Now you wait and watch, Jane will show you how much she loves you when you two go home?"

(Jane says)

"Helen don't worry I'll see that my husband does not leave the room for seven days?"

(Dr. Anthony King says)

"Jane please doesn't try to break the world record?"

(Everyone laughs, and then Dr. Barry Johnson says)

"Jane I hope that you or Mike are not hospitalized after seven days?"

(Dr. Robert Stanford says)

"Don't worry Mike our hospital bed will be always free for you and Jane?"

(Bob and Madeleine comes there with a bouquet so big that it is the same height of Jane, on the bouquet there are gifts tied to it, Bob and Madeleine gives the bouquet to Jane and Dr. Mike Tyler, and then Bob and Madeleine says)

"All the best"

(Jane and Mike say together)

"Thank you"

(Helen tells Bob and Madeleine)

"First time I am seeing such a beautiful gift?"

(Jane tells bob and Madeleine)

"I am really touched by your gift?"

(Then Carol says)

"Why are you all not dancing?"

(Dr. Robert Stanford says)

"I was waiting for you Carol?"

(Carol smiles and says)

"Me! That's wonderful chief; I may steal you from Doris?"

(Dr. Robert Stanford says)

"A palmist had told me that I am going to marry twice in this birth?"

(Everybody laughs and then they all go on the dance floor and starts dancing on the background slow song number, Dr. John Hopes is holding Helen very tightly towards him, and then Helen asks)

"Are you going to chock me to death with love?"

"I want to kill you so I'll be free again?"

"I hope you have not found any girlfriend?"

"Someone wanted to marry me?"

(Helen is shocked, and then she asks)

"What do you mean?"

"Joan Banks asked me to marry her"

"Joan Banks! Who's Joan Banks?"

"She is a film actor and I am treating her in our hospital for stomach injury"

"Does she know you before she came to the hospital?"

"No, I met her the first time in the hospital?"

"And she wanted to marry you?"

"Yeah"

"She is a dangerous woman, please keep your distance from her?"

"Yeah, I have told Dr. Barry Johnson to handle her case?"

"Good for you"

"You did not feel jealous?"

"Come on John grow up?"

"You did not feel even insecure?"

"I believe in destiny? So I leave everything to destiny?"

"Helen, you are one of a kind?"

"Do you want to waste time talking?"

"Oh! So you want some action?"

(Dr. John Hopes kisses tightly on the lips of Helen and then he asks)

"You want to return my kiss?"

(Helen kisses Dr. john Hopes on the lips)

(Dr. Robert Stanford is dancing with Carol, and then Dr. Robert Stanford says)

"Carol let's call everybody and we can dance in a circle?"

"That's a good idea?"

(Carol and Dr. Robert Stanford go and bring Helen and Dr. John hopes, Rosalie and Dr. Anthony King, Martha and Dr. Barry Johnson, Jane and Dr. Mike Tyler, they all make a circle and dance round and round putting there hands on each other shoulders, this goes on for five minutes until the music gets over, and then Jane says)

"Attention everybody please I want your attention?"

(Everybody looks at Jane, and then Jane says)

"Now my friend Helen will sing a song only for me, everybody give her a big hand?"

(Everybody claps; Helen takes the mike and starts singing)

"Come rain or storm, we are friends forever,

Come rain or storm, we are friends forever,

My heart bleeds to see you go today,

The memories fill my heart with sorrow,

The little time we had together, will haunt me forever,

Come rain or storm we are friends forever,

You are to me a sister,

You are to me a friend,

From tomorrow I won't see you,

But your shadow will remain with me,

Come rain or storm we are friends forever"

(Crying Jane runs towards Helen whose eyes are filled with tears, Jane hugs Helen tightly and they both cry, Rosalie And Martha with tears in their eyes go and hug Jane and Helen)

(Dr. Mike Tyler has Jane in his arms and he comes in to his house, Dr. John Hopes, Helen, Dr. Anthony King, Rosalie, Dr. Barry Johnson, Martha, Dr. Robert Stanford, Doris son Robert, Carol, Carol's sister and her husband enter Dr. Mike Tyler's house, Dr. Mike Tyler puts Jane down, and then Jane says)

"Thank you everybody for the love and support"

(Helen smiles and says)

"That's a nice way of saying good night to all of us?"

(Everyone laughs, and then Dr. John hopes says)

"I have never seen a honeymoon in my life?"

(Helen says)

"Don't worry John you are going to witness the full honeymoon tonight"

(Dr. Mike Tyler asks in a surprised tone)

"You mean to say you all are going to watch our honeymoon show live?"

(Rosalie tells Dr. Mike Tyler)

"Then what are friends for?"

(Dr. Anthony King says)

"Yes, before our marriage we all will get experience that what happens on the honeymoon night?"

(Jane says)

"Look all of you call me up in the morning and I'll tell you the full scene, ok?"

(Martha says)

"Not ok Jane? We know that after today you and Dr. Mike Tyler are not going to take any call for seven days?"

(Again everyone laughs, Dr. Mike Tyler says)

"Come on friends this is a private show?"

(Dr. Robert Stanford says)

"Don't worry Mike I will close your mother in-law's eyes?"

(Again everyone laughs, and then Carol says)

"Look they are not going to do anything tonight, because I am going to sleep with my daughter Jane?"

(Jane asks Carol)

"Mother you also?"

(Carol looks at everyone and then she says)

"I don't want to see my daughter suffering?"

(Again everyone laughs, and then Jane asks))

"Mother! Then how was I born?"

"Carol smiles and tells Jane)

"I don't remember? Look I forget what I have eaten last night and you were born a long time back? How am I going to remember that??"

(Again everyone laughs, and then Jane smiles and says)

"Ok, you want to watch a free show?"

(Jane goes and takes out the coat from Dr. Mike Tyler's body, then she takes out the shirt from Dr. Mike Tyler's body, and then she removes the pant from Mike Tyler's body, Dr. Mike Tyler now has only short boxer shorts on him, and then Jane says)

"Ok everybody I will count three then I'll remove Mike's Boxer shorts? One? Two?"

(Jane puts both her hands on Mike's boxer shorts, and then Helen smiles and says)

"Wait Jane, we all don't want Dr. Mike Tyler to feel ashamed on seeing us tomorrow?"

(Jane says)

"Don't worry? Mike will get used to it being shameless?"

(Dr. Robert Stanford says)

"Ok Jane you win, everybody let's go?"

(Helen, Rosalie and Martha hug Jane, and then Dr. John Hopes tells Mike)

"Mike you have seven more nights ahead of you so doesn't get tired tonight?"

(Everyone laughs and goes away from the door, Dr. Mike Tyler closes the door and then he asks Jane)

"Jane you were really going to take my boxer shorts off?"

"Yeah Mike?"

"Oh my god! I would have felt so ashamed?"

(Jane laughs and hugs Mike, Mike lifts Jane and takes her towards the bed, then Mike puts Jane on the bed, they kiss and start making love, and then after a minute Mike asks Jane)

"Jane where would you like to go for our honeymoon?"

"Mike I want to tell you something"

"What?"

"How many dollars we will have to spend for our Honeymoon?"

"About ten thousand dollars"

"Please I want to suggest something?"

"Come on Jane you are my better half now? Say what you want to say?"

"If we spend our honeymoon in this house you won't mind?"

"No I won't mind, but why?"

"Look Dr. Barry Johnson is in trouble? He has to pay people money that his father had borrowed? Now if we help him with ten thousand dollars?

"Oh! That's very nice of you Jane! I'll be more than happy to help Dr. Barry Johnson, but will he take money from us?"

"You leave that to me, I'll handle it, and tomorrow everyone is coming here for dinner some how I'll make Dr. Barry Johnson agree to take the money?"

"No problem, I'll take out the money from the bank tomorrow and give it to you"

"Now I am going to give you love worth ten thousand dollars"

(Jane starts taking of her clothes)

(In the morning in the hospital Wisdom is talking on the phone at the Get-Well hospital reception counter, and then Wisdom says on the phone)

"I am telling you that Dr. Mike Tyler is on leave"

(Helen comes their she looks at Wisdom and shakes her head saying hello, Wisdom smiles at her then Wisdom says on the phone)

"Look Dr. Mike Tyler has married and he is on leave for his honeymoon, no I can't disturb him, can I suggest you another doctor? Ok? Then have a nice day"

(Wisdom keeps the receiver of the phone down, and then Helen asks Wisdom)

"Wisdom today you were talking on the phone so nicely, but sometimes you just forget and talk nonsense?"

"It is because of my brain not working properly sometimes?"

"What is wrong with your brain?"

"I myself don't know, many years back in Africa my full family was killed by my relatives, I survived and came to America"

"Why don't you get your brain checked?"

"I would rather die than get my brain checked"

"You don't want get your brain checked! Why?"

"Helen, now I don't know what is wrong with my brain but if tomorrow I come to know that something is wrong with my brain than everyday the tension would kill me?"

"I understand your point, but why didn't you come for Jane's wedding?"

"I forgot"

"Oh!"

"You must be missing Jane?"

(Tears come in the eyes of Helen, and then Wisdom says)

"I am sorry, I upset you?"

"It's ok"

"Oh Helen the new patient Joan Banks asked for you"

"I also want to meet her, which room is she in?"

"Room number twenty"

"Thanks"

"The way she talked to me like I am her servant, Helen I think she is not a nice woman?"

"Don't worry Wisdom, I know how to tackle these kind of woman?"

(Helen turns and goes away, and then Wisdom says to himself)

"I hope Helen gives it to her where it hurts the most?"

(Joan Banks is lying in her room talking on her mobile phone, and then she says)

"Mom I want that car, I don't care how much it costs, now you listen to me mom what I want I always get it in the end so please don't bore me with your stupid advice"

(Helen comes in to the room; Joan Banks looks at her and then she says on the mobile phone)

"Get the money from my producer ok? I am fine you worry about yourself"

(Joan banks switches off the mobile and then she asks Helen)

"If you have come to take my autograph then I am not in the mood to give it to you"

"Why should I want to take your autograph?"

(Joan is surprised, and then she says)

"I don't like people staring at me, get out"

"There is nothing in your face to stare at?"

(Joan gets angry and sits up on the bed and then she asks)

"Then what the fuck do you want?"

"Mind your language please?"

(Joan banks really get angry, and then she shouts)

"Buzz off or I'll call the chief?"

"It's a free country, you can call whom you want?"

(Joan Banks starts dialing the numbers on her mobile, and then she says)

"Hey chief some fucking nurse is irritating me, tell her to get out before I beat her up"

(Helen tells Joan Banks)

"Mind your language please?"

(Joan Banks tells Helen)

"Your chief wants to talk to you"

(Joan Banks gives the mobile to Helen; Helen takes the Mobile then wipes the mobile with her nurse uniform, and then Helen says)

"Yes chief?"

(Helen listens to the voice of chief and then Helen says)

"Chief in the first place I did not come to the room of I even don't know the name? Wisdom on the reception counter told me that some patient wanted to meet me in room number twenty? Ok chief?

(Helen gives the mobile back to Joan Banks, and then Joan Banks asks the chief on the mobile)

"Who is she? Oh! Helen?"

(Joan Banks switches of her mobile, then she asks Helen)

"Why did not you say that you were the bitch who thinks that she is in love with Dr. John Hopes?"

"I never think, I am always sure"

"Sure! I think that it is a one sided love? Dr. John Hopes loves you?

"You better ask this question to Dr. John Hopes?"

"You are a smart bitch"

"I think you don't know the real meaning of a bitch?"

"So you know! Tell me?"

"A bitch is the one who tries to come in between two lovers"

"A fight of words you want? You will get plenty from me, see yourself in the mirror and see me?"

"But you're not worth looking at?"

"People look at me and say what a beautiful woman?"

"But I have heard that beauty is skin deep?"

(Joan Banks has a wicked smile on her face, she tells Helen)

"I am going to steal your lover Dr. John Hopes from you, you better prepare yourself?"

"Relationship are made in heavens, but you are so rotten that I think you will rot in hell?"

"Ok? How much rotten I am you will see it in a few days and you don't know who my mother is?"

"Why! Don't you know who your mother is?"

"Shut up you good for nothing slut"

"Slut? Sluts are woman's who try to poke their nose in other people's lives?" Sluts are woman who try to wreak other people's homes? Sluts are women who try to ruin other people happiness?"

"How I am going to wreak your life you wait and watch? As you have hurt me, now my mother and father will hurt you?"

"Everyone has seen your mother and father fighting like a cat and a dog outside your room, what a scene it was?"

(Helen smile at Joan Banks and then she goes out of the room, Joan Banks is so angry that she bangs her mobile on the floor)

(In the hospital canteen Rosalie and Martha are having there breakfast, Helen comes and sits down on the chair beside them, seeing Helen angry face Rosalie asks her)

"Helen! What's wrong?"

(Helen says)

"That new patient Joan Banks called me and insulted me?"

(Rosalie says)

"Yeah, even nurse Flora was saying that Joan Banks behaved very nasty with her?"

(Martha tells Helen)

"Helen you should have insulted her back?"

"I did, I also insulted her, but she was using foul Language?"

(Martha says)

What say Rosalie, shall we both go and give her our piece of our mind?

(Helen says)

"No please don't do that, she had called the chief on her mobile?"

(Martha asks Helen)

"And what did the chief say?"

"Chief did not say anything, but I told chief that Joan Banks only called me to her room?"

(Rosalie says)

"Before she creates more trouble somebody has to do something?"

(Helen says)

"We will talk with chief when we go for dinner in the night at Jane's house?"

(Rosalie says)

"Ok, now Helen you just relax and have a coffee, Bob please bring a coffee for Helen?"

(Bob says)

"One coffee coming right up"

(In the house of Jane and Dr. Mike Tyler everyone is sitting down on the floor about to eat their dinner, and then Dr. Robert Stanford says)

"We pray before we eat"

(Dr. Robert Stanford, Robert, Dr. John hopes, Helen. Dr. Anthony King, Rosalie, Dr. Barry Johnson, Martha, Dr. Mike Tyler, Jane and Jane's mother Carol are sitting on the floor of Dr. Mike Tyler's house in the living room, all fold their hands, and then Dr. Robert Stanford says)

"Lord Jesus Christ we thank you for the food we share tonight, we thank you for the love and the support of our family and friends, heavenly father we ask this blessing for this newly married couple, amen"

(Everyone makes a Jesus Christ Cross sign on his or her chests, and then Jane says)

"Thank you chief"

(Dr. Robert Stanford says)

"God bless you both"

(Dr. Mike Tyler says)

"God bless you chief and all who are sitting in this house"

(Dr. John Hopes says)

"The food smells so good?"

"John, my mother cooked the food"

(Dr. John Hopes smiles and says)

"Oh! I will have to borrow your mother for a week after my wedding?"

(Everyone laughs, and then Helen tells Carol)

"I think I have to learn to cook like you mother?"

(Carol says)

"Anytime Helen anytime, I wish we could all stay together and I would cook food for everyone in the house?"

(Dr. Robert Stanford says)

"Staying together! That's not a bad idea Carol?"

(Dr. Barry Johnson says)

"But you all will have to excuse Martha and me, we can't marry for some time?"

(Carol asks)

"Barry you and Martha can't marry for sometime! Why?"

"My father has left a debt on me, which I have to pay every month?"

(Carol asks Dr. Barry Johnson)

"What is the amount?"

"One hundred thousand dollars"

(Carol looks at everyone and then she tells Dr. Barry Johnson)

"We all can help you out?"

(Dr. Barry Johnson says)

"Please, no, I will pay up my own debt"

(Jane tells Dr. Barry Johnson)

"That means you don't think we are your friends?"

(Dr. Barry Johnson looks at everyone and then he says)

"You all are my only friends?"

(Jane tells Dr. Barry Johnson))

"Then your problem is our problem also?"

(Dr. Robert Stanford says)

"Barry, we are all family? So we are all for one and one for all, right?

(Dr. Barry John son says)

"Right chief"

(Dr. Robert Stanford says)

"Then you have to listen to all of us? Now I can give you twenty thousand dollars?"

(Dr. Mike Tyler tells Dr. Barry Johnson)

"Jane and I can give you ten thousand dollars right now?"

(Jane gives the ten thousand dollars to Dr. Barry Johnson, and then Dr. John Hopes tell Dr. Barry Johnson))

"Helen and I can give you ten thousand dollars?"

(Dr. Anthony King tells Dr. Barry Johnson)

"Rosalie and I can give you ten thousand dollars?"

(Dr. Barry Johnson tells Dr. Anthony King)

"Anthony you still have to get your four sisters married in Africa? I can't take money from you?"

(Rosalie says)

"Dr. Barry Johnson your problem is a dangerous problem? These gangsters can do harm to you? First we have to solve your problem?"

(Carol says)

"I can give you fifty thousand dollars Dr. Barry Johnson?"

(Martha looks at everyone, and then she says)

"That's not fair? You all need the money also?"

(Carol tells Martha)

"As they say a friend in need is a friend indeed? Martha our bond of friendship is more than the one hundred thousand dollars?"

(Dr. Barry Johnson eyes are filled with tears, and then he says in a chocked voice)

"You all are giving me one hundred thousand dollars? How will I be able to repay you all?"

(Carol goes to Dr. Barry Johnson and then she tells him)

"You can thank us all by giving a kiss to your mother?"

(Dr. Barry Johnson gives a kiss to Carol on her cheek and hugs her, and then Dr. Robert Stanford says)

"Now Dr. Barry Johnson and Martha there will be no discussion on this money topic and before the emotion gets the better of us? Let's eat?"

(Everyone puts the food in his or her plates, and then they start eating, and then Dr. Robert Stanford asks Helen)

"Helen, why did Joan Banks want to see you?"

(Helen says)

"She wanted to know why Dr. John Hopes is in love with a woman like me?"

(Dr. Robert Stanford gets angry and then he says)

"What has Joan Banks got to do with your personal life?

(Helen tells Dr. Robert Stanford)

"That's what I told her? That this question about Dr. John Hopes wanting to marry me you better ask Dr. John Hopes? But she started using foul language?"

(Dr. Robert Stanford says)

"I'll talk to Joan Banks tomorrow and tell her never to come to our hospital again?"

(Dr. John Hopes tells dr. Robert Stanford)

"That's why I told Dr. Barry Johnson to check her everyday? I also feel that she is a mental?"

(Dr. Barry Johnson tells Dr. Robert Stanford)

"She talks rubbish with the hospital staff and she thinks that everyone is her servant?"

(Dr. Robert Stanford says)

"I will deal with Joan Banks? Helen even if she calls you? Don't go to her room?"

(Helen says)

"Ok"

(Dr. Robert Stanford says)

"Let's talk about something else?"

(Dr. John Hopes smiles and then he says)

"Like when Dr. Barry Johnson and Martha are getting married?"

(Carol says)

"Yes now the wedding bell should ring in the house of Dr. Barry Johnson?"

(Everyone says together)

"Yes"

(Dr. Robert Stanford says)

"Look Dr. Barry Johnson I don't want to loose a good nurse like Martha after marriage? So you promise that after marriage you will let Martha work in the hospital?"

Dr. Barry Johnson smiles and then he says)

"I promise"

(Dr. Robert Stanford says)

"Dr. John Hopes what about you and Helen?

(Dr. John hopes says)

"Helen and me have given each other a year? But if we decide to get married before the year is over then chief you will be the first one to know?"

(Dr. Robert Stanford says)

"Dr. John Hopes you will also let Helen work after marriage?" After marriage Helen will work but I will retire?"

(Everyone is surprised, and then Dr. Robert Stanford asks Dr. John Hopes)

"You will retire! Why?"

(Dr. John Hopes smiles and then he says)

"I have to take care of Helen's babies?"

(Everyone laughs, and then Carol asks Dr. John Hopes)

"John do you know how to change baby diapers?"

(Dr. John Hopes asks)

"Carol can teach me?"

(Again everyone laughs, and then Dr. Robert Stanford says)

"What about you Dr. Anthony King?"

(Dr. Anthony King says)

"Chief you know that I have to get my four sisters married first? It's a promise I have made that I have to fulfill? After that I will marry Rosalie?"

(Dr. Robert Stanford says)

"God will fulfill your wish?

(Dr. Anthony King says)

"Yes chief if fulfill my wish then I'll marry Rosalie the same day my sister's get married?"

(Dr. Robert Stanford says)

"Well we all hope for the best Dr. Anthony King? Carol your idea of staying all together in one house has appealed to me so much that I want this idea to be successful?"

(Dr. Barry Johnson is driving the car, Martha is sitting beside him, and then Martha asks Dr. Barry Johnson)

"Barry where are we going?"

"Well our one hundred thousand dollars load has been lifted from my head today?" I just want to go to the river and relax?"

"What a good idea? But are we only going to relax at the river?"

"Well let us get married I will show you what lovemaking is?

"I am an expert in love making Barry? You will lose?"

"we will see who floors whom in love making?"

"I thing I am going to love this love making match after our wedding? And suppose you lose, then?"

"Well then the rest of our lives you will the boss of the house? I will do whatever you tell me?"

"Oh! That's great?"

(Dr. Barry Johnson stops his car near the river, and then they both get down from the car and go and sit on the bench, Martha puts her head on the shoulder of Dr. Barry Johnson, Dr. Barry Johnson puts his hand on the shoulder of Martha, and then Dr. Barry Johnson says)

"Tomorrow we will discuss our wedding plans?"

"Oh Barry I love you"

"How many children should we have?"

(Martha is so surprised that she kisses Dr. Barry Johnson on the lips and then she says)

"Quite a change has come in to you?"

"Today I think the world is a better place to live in?"

"Now our troubles and worries are over?"

" We don't think so"

(Dr. Barry Johnson and Martha are shocked to see four men standing around them, they all have liquor bottles in their hands, and then Dr. Barry Johnson asks)

"What do you want?"

(One man says)

"We want the woman?"

"You can only have her upon my dead body?"

"So be it"

(The first man tries to hold Martha, Martha pushes the man, the man falls down on the ground, the second man takes out a big hunting knife, and then he says)

"We don't want to hurt you?" But we will take the woman?"

(Dr. Barry Johnson tells the four men's)

"Anyone who tries to touch her will die?"

(All four comes towards Martha, Dr. Barry Johnson who knows boxing, punches all four of them, and then third man says)

"So you are going to put up a fight?"

(Dr. Barry Johnson gets in front of Martha, all the four throw down their bottles and jump on Dr. Barry Johnson, a fight takes place, the person who was holding the knife thrusts the knife in to the stomach of Dr. Barry Johnson, the knife goes fully inside the stomach of Dr. Barry Johnson, Dr. Barry Johnson falls down on the ground, and then Martha shouts)

"Oh my god! Barry? Barry? Help? Somebody help?

(On seeing this one man tells the second man)

"You stupid bastard, you were supposed to scare him? I think you have killed him?

(All the four men run away)

(Helen and Rosalie are sitting outside the operation theatre, Jane comes running with Dr. Mike Tyler, and then Jane asks)

"How is Dr. Barry Johnson?"

(Helen and Rosalie run and hug Jane and then they start crying, and then Jane says)

"I know it is hard on us to believe that Dr. Barry John son was stabbed by a knife? But please tell me how is Dr. Barry Johnson?"

(Helen wipes her tears and then she tells Jane)

"The doctors are operating on him"

(Helen again starts crying, Jane looks here and there and then she asks)

"Where is Martha?"

(Rosalie tells Jane)

"She lying in a room unconscious"

(Jane sits down beside Helen and Rosalie. Dr. Mike Tyler paces up and down, Dr. Robert Stanford opens the operation theatre door, behind him Dr. John Hopes and Dr. Anthony King come out, and then Dr. Mike Tyler asks)

"How is Dr. Barry Johnson?"

(Dr. Robert Stanford, Dr. John Hopes and Dr. Anthony King have tears in their eyes, and then crying Dr. Robert Stanford says)

(We could not save Dr. Barry Johnson, he died on the operation table"

(Dr. Mike Tyler says)

"My god! No? No?"

(Helen, Rosalie and Jane start crying, and then Dr. John Hopes says)

(Dr. John Hopes says)

"What will we say to Martha after she regains consciousness?"

(Dr. Anthony King says)

"It will be a shock to Martha when she finds out that Dr. Barry Johnson is dead?"

(Dr. Robert Stanford wipes his tears and then he says)

"Yes, but we have to tell her the truth?"

(Martha regains consciousness and opens her eyes; Dr. Robert Stanford, Dr. John Hopes, Dr. Anthony King, Dr. Mike Tyler, Helen, Rosalie and Jane are standing beside Martha's bed, and then Martha asks)

"You all have come to see me! Thank you? Please I want to see Barry?"

(Everyone looks at each other, and then Dr. Robert Stanford tells Martha)

"Yes we will take you to him, please somebody help her?"

(Helen, Rosalie and Jane help Martha get down from the bed, and then they all go out of the room)

(Dr. Barry Johnson is lying on the bed, everyone comes in to the room, and Martha goes near Dr. Barry Johnson and takes his hand in her hand and then she says)

"Thanks Barry for saving me, Barry? Barry? Why is your hand so cold?"

(Martha looks at everyone; Dr. Robert Stanford goes towards Martha and then he tells her)

"Martha, Dr. Barry Johnson is no more"

Martha—No more?

(Martha is unconscious, she falls but Dr. Robert Stanford catches her)

(The coffin of Dr. Barry Johnson is inside the grave, the priest let's three hand-full of earth fall onto the coffin, and then the priest says)

"You gave him life. Receive him in peace and give Through Jesus Christ, a joyful resurrection"

(Dr. Robert Stanford, Dr. John hopes, Dr. Anthony King, Dr. Mike Tyler, Helen, Rosalie, Jane and Martha let hand-full of earth fall on the coffin with tears in their eyes, and then the priest says)

"Lord god, our father in heaven, lord god, the son, and savior of the world, lord god, the Holy Spirit, have mercy on us. At the moment of death, and on the last day, save us, Merciful and gracious lord god"

(Martha is unconscious and she falls down)

(In the apartment Helen, Rosalie, Jane, Dr. Robert Stanford, Dr. Mike Tyler, Dr. John Hopes, and dr. Anthony King, are sitting on the sofa, everyone has tears in their eyes, Martha is sitting looking down on the floor, and then Helen tells Martha)

"Martha in this moment of grief, all we can do is lend you our support"

(Dr. Robert Stanford says)

"Martha, please now you have to control your tears? Dr. Barry Johnson is gone but his memories will always remain in our hearts forever?"

(Martha looks at everyone, and then crying she says)

"I know he is no more and he is not going to come back? But I am
   not able to accept the truth?"

*(Dr. John hopes goes and puts his hand on the shoulder of Martha,
and then he tells her)*

"Time heals all wounds. God is great"

(Martha tells Dr. John Hopes)

"But how am I going to heal the wounds that have wounded my
   heart? I know nobody can help me heal my wounds? But how can
   you forget the person whom you had loved more than yourself?

(Dr. Anthony King tells Martha)

"Martha we understand your problem? But life has to move on? It is
   a circle of life and death? For that no one has the answer?"

(Martha says)

"Why did it happen to my Barry?"

(Rosalie says)

"Martha please? Nobody knows the answer to what god does?"

(Martha crying gets up, and then she says)

"Yes I know? But my life story has come to an end?"

*(Helen, Jane, and Rosalie get up and hold Martha in their arms and
they start crying, Dr. John Hopes wants to go to them but Dr. Robert
Stanford holds the hand of Dr. John Hopes and stops him saying no
by nodding his head)*

*(Tora banks and Fred Banks are sitting in the cabin of Dr. Robert
Stanford, and then Tora Banks asks her husband)*

"Why is Dr. Robert Stanford taking so long? I have an appointment?"

(Fred Banks gets angry, and then he asks)

"Why are you asking me this question?"

"I was not talking to you"

"I did not know that the walls of this room listen to you?"

"Why don't you mind your own business?"

(Dr. Robert Stanford who is standing near the door asks)

"If you two have finished your argument? I would like to come in?

(On seeing Dr. Robert Stanford Fred Banks gets up and extends his hand and then he says)

"Good morning Dr. Robert Stanford, I am Joan's Father, Fred Banks"

(Dr. Robert Stanford shakes hand with Fred Banks and then he says)

"Good morning sir"

(Tora Banks tells Dr. Robert Stanford in an irritating tone)

"Please doctor say what you want to say and make it quick? I have an appointment?"

(Dr. Robert Stanford gets angry and then he shows his hand towards his cabin door and then he tells Tora Banks)

"Ma'am if you want you can go? I'll talk with Mr. Fred Banks?"

(Tora Banks says in a low voice)

"No I'll wait"

(Dr. Robert Stanford goes and sits down on his chair, and then he says)

"I'll come straight to the point, your daughter Joan's behavior with the doctors and the nurses of this hospital is inappropriate?"

(Tora Banks says)

"Oh it must be?"

(Dr. Robert Stanford raises his hand and stops Tora Banks saying anything further, and then he says)

"I have not finished talking yet? Secondly, Joan Banks is using foul language with the employees of this hospital? Yes ma'ams now tell me what you wanted to say?

(Tora Banks says)

"She must be irritated because of her wound in the stomach?"

(Dr. Robert Stanford shouts)

"That is no excuse? She even told one of our nurses that why is a doctor in love with her and she even told the nurse that she would break their relationship and marry the doctor? I don't think that her stomach wound is the reason for your daughter to say that?"

(Fred Banks says)

"Doctor I apologize for my daughter's behavior?"

(Tora Banks tells Dr. Robert Stanford)

"The nurse might be lying?"

(Dr. Robert Stanford gets angry and he gets up and asks Tora Banks)

"And why would the nurse lie?"

(Tora Banks says)

"She must be jealous of my daughter's being rich and famous?"

(Dr. points a finger at Tora Banks and then he tells her)

"Look ma'am here in this hospital nobody cares who the patient is?"

(Tora Banks)

"Then the nurse must have instigated my daughter to be rude?"

(Dr. Robert Stanford tells Tora Banks)

"Then I think that you better take your daughter to another hospital?"

(Fred Banks pleads with Dr. Robert Stanford)

"Please doctor we are very sorry? I'll tell my daughter to apologize to the nurse?"

(Tora Banks gets up and then she says)

"I can't tolerate my daughter being insulted? I think I will go?"

(Tora Banks gets up, and then Dr. Robert Stanford tells Tora Banks)

"This attitude of yours you can show it in the studios where your daughter is shooting? Nobody cares who or what you are in this hospital?"

(Tora Banks turns and goes out of the cabin, and then Fred Banks tells Dr. Robert Stanford)

I am sorry? My wife has spoiled my daughter?"

"And sir you are Joan's father? Why did not you stop your wife from spoiling your daughter?"

(Fred Banks sits down on the chair, and then he says)

"I was never the man of the house"

(Fred Banks lowers his head, Dr. Robert Stanford sits down on the chair, and then Dr. Robert Stanford says)

"I understand your point? But mark my words one day you and your wife will repent because of your daughter? Please I request you to take away your daughter from this hospital today itself?"

"Please doctor forgives my daughter's mistake? What would you have done if Joan were your daughter?

"I would have thrown her out of my house?"

(Fred Banks gets up and goes out of the cabin. And then Dr. Robert Stanford says to himself)

"It is true? A woman makes a man or breaks a man?"

(Joan Banks is sitting on her bed talking on her mobile, and then Joan Banks says)

"Come on Sarah grow up, you have used Rod for a long time, don't you get bored going out with the same man day after day?

(Fred Banks comes in to the room, and then Joan Banks says on her mobile)

"I'll talk to you later?"

(Joan Banks switches of her mobile and then she asks Fred Banks)

"Hi dad, how are you?"

(Fred Banks sits down on a chair beside the bed, and then he says)

"Not well"

"Why! Did you have a fight with mom?"

"Dr. Robert Stanford has told us to take you to another hospital?"

"Why?"

"Because of your bad behavior with the employees of this hospital"

"Oh! Nobody can throw me out of this hospital?"

"They can Joan, in your sub consciousness you were saying mom don't make me angrily otherwise I'll hurt myself? This Dr. John Hopes told your mom and me, he warned us that he would give this statement to the police or the press?"

"Dr. John Hopes! Ok dad you don't worry I'll take care of everything, ok?"

"When you say that then I get really worried"

"Dad, you know I always win in the end?"

"Please Joan don't do something that I'll be ashamed off?"

"Nobody can insult me and get away with it?"

(Fred Banks shakes his head and gets up from the chair and then he goes out of the room, and then Joan Banks says)

"Your days of happiness are over Dr. John Hopes"

(In the hospital corridor Joan Banks runs and crashes in to a glass door, Joan Banks had covered her face with her hands before crashing in to the glass door, Joan Banks falls down on the ground, the employees of the hospital comes running and picks up Joan Banks and takes her away)

(Dr. Robert Stanford is sitting in his cabin; Tora Banks comes in to the cabin with a man, Dr. Robert Stanford looks at Tora Banks and then he asks)

"Yes?"

(Tora Banks looks angrily at Dr. Robert Stanford, and then she says)

"I will sue you and your hospital?"

(Dr. Robert Stanford gets up from his chair, and then he asks angrily)

"For what?"

"You told my husband to take my daughter from this hospital and my stupid husband went and told my daughter, my daughter was coming to you to apologize but as she is very weak she banged into the glass door of your hospital?"

"Your daughter banged into the glass door? So how is the hospital responsible?"

(The man who had come with Tora Banks tells Dr. Robert Stanford)

"I am Rod Brampton and I am the attorney of Tora Banks and she can sue you and your hospital?"

(Dr. Robert Stanford is so angry that he bangs his hand on the table, and then he says)

"Then go and sue me and my hospital? I'll call the press reporters and give them the full story of how a mother instigated her daughter to take her own life and the witness is Dr. John Hopes?"

(Tora Banks tells Dr. Robert Stanford)

"Nobody is going to believe you?"

"When any operation is done we record each and every operation for new interns who come to this hospital? If you want I can call the press reporters and you can watch the tape with the press reporters? And Mr. Rod Brampton I will personally put a case against you and Tora Banks?"

(Mr. Rod Brampton asks Dr. Robert Stanford)

"Doctor how can you put up a case against me?"

(Dr. Robert Stanford says)

"I will put up a case against Tora banks for instigating her daughter to hurt herself and I will put up a case against you for putting up a false against me and my hospital?"

(Mr. Rod Brampton looks at Tora Banks and then he tells Dr. Robert Stanford)

"Oh! I am sorry for what I said doctor? Ma'am Tora I don't want to get involve in your matter?"

(Rod Brampton goes away from the cabin, and then Dr. Robert Stanford tells Tora Banks)

"Now if you disturb me again? I'll see to it that you go to jail? Now get the hell out of my cabin before I throw you out?"

(Tora Banks gets up and goes out of the cabin)

(Joan Banks has bandages over her hands and body and is lying on the bed, Tora Banks comes in to the room and then she asks Joan Banks)

"Does it hurt too much Joan?"

"When you injure yourself then the pain is always very sweet"

"You mean to say that you purposely banged yourself in to the glass door?"

"Yes mom"

"But why?"

"To stay in this hospital and take revenge"

"But you could have disfigured your face?"

"I am not that stupid, I covered my face before I banged in to the glass door"

"You are my girl; the revenge part should be very good? You have to take revenge for yourself and me also?

"I am like you mom, Dr. John Hopes will curse the day he was born"

"I even want to get back at that son of a bitch Dr. Robert Stanford, but?"

"Mom don't, the bad publicity would ruin you and me, now would you mind getting out of my room?"

"Ok, I know in your mind you are thinking of a wicked plan?"

"Just buzz off mom"

(Tora Banks goes out of the room closing the door behind her, and then Joan Banks says)

"As they say if you can't trap a person by your beauty you use your brain and my brain says I should emotionally trap that son of a bitch Dr. John Hopes"

(Dr. Robert Stanford, Dr. Peter Liao and Dr. Steve Wayne are in the room of Doris in the hospital. Doris is unconscious and lying on the bed, and then Dr. Peter Liao tells Dr. Robert Stanford)

"Dr. Robert Stanford Doris is responding to the treatment we are giving her"

(Dr. Robert Stanford says)

"Thanks Dr. Peter Liao, it is a relief to hear that"

(Dr. Steve Wayne tells Dr. Robert Stanford)

"But still we are not hundred percent sure what will be the final result?"

(Dr. Robert Stanford looks at Doris and then he says)

"I understand that, I know you two are doing your best"

(Dr. Peter Liao says)

"When the patient is thinking in his mind that he wants to live then the medicine also works"

(Dr. Steve Wayne says)

"Yeah, Dr. Peter Liao is right, Doris also knows that she also has to fight this battle and win it"

(Dr. Robert Stanford says)

"In Doris mind she must be thinking about our son Robert?"

(Dr. Peter Liao looks here and there and then he asks Dr. Robert Stanford)

"Shall we go out of the room?"

(Dr. Robert Stanford shows his towards the door, and then he says)

"Sure? After you doctors"

(Dr. Peter Liao, Dr. Steve Wayne and Dr. Robert Stanford comes out of the room, they start walking into the corridor of the hospital, then Dr. Peter Liao Asks Dr. Robert Stanford)

"Where is your son Robert?"

(Dr. Robert Stanford smiles and then he says)

"He has gone to school"

(Dr. Steve Wayne says)

"Dr. Robert Stanford we really respect you for what you are doing for Doris? I don't want to get personal but giving a child a father's name is really great?"

(Dr. Peter Liao says)

"Yes, Dr. Steve Wayne is right? Not many people have the guts like you Dr. Robert Stanford to give a name to somebody else son?"

(Dr. Robert Stanford says)

"A power comes in to you automatically when love is there and your heart is in it?"

(Dr. Steve Wayne smiles and then he says)

"Dr. Peter Liao, after we both retire we should write a book on Dr. Robert Stanford?"

(They all laugh, and then Dr. Peter Liao says)

"Yes and if our book is made in to a movie? Then that movie will be the biggest hit of the year?"

(Dr. Robert Stanford says)

"You two Doctors have really boosted my ego? Thanks to you both?"

(Dr. Peter Liao says)

"Dr. Robert it is our honor to be associate with a good human like you? We shall take your leave now Dr. Robert Stanford?"

"Dr. Robert Stanford"

"Ok and thank you so much for taking out so much time for Doris? I really appreciate?"

(Dr. Steve Wayne says)

"No problem Dr. Robert Stanford or as they say in America nice people no problem?"

(They again all laugh, Dr. Robert Stanford shakes hand with Dr. Peter Liao and Dr. Steve Wayne, Dr. Peter Liao and Dr. Steve Barnes goes towards their car, Dr. Robert Stanford looks up and then he says)

"God please Doris now needs your blessings?"

(Then Dr. Robert Stanford turns and goes inside the hospital)

(Helen and Rosalie are sitting in the canteen of the hospital, Bob brings two cups of coffee and puts it down on the table, and then Bob asks)

"How is Martha?"

(Helen tells Bob)

"She has not gotten over that Dr. Barry Johnson is dead? So Jane has taken Martha with her to live in her house"

(Bob puts his hand on the shoulder of Helen, and then he says)

"That's was very nice of Jane to take Martha with her to her house? But time will heal all the wounds of Martha"

(Helen says)

"I hope you are right Bob"

"Those four bastards who stabbed Dr. Barry Johnson should be hanged when they are caught?"

(Rosalie tells Bob)

"This country does not spare anybody who is a criminal?"

(Bob says)

"Today Amana is being discharged from the hospital?"

(Helen gets up, and then she says)

"I forgot about Amana? Come on Rosalie let's go?"

(Bob says)

"I can't say goodbye to Amana? I won't come?"

(Rosalie says)

"We understand Bob, come on Helen, let's go?"

(Rosalie and Helen leave the coffee mugs on the table and get up, and then go out of the canteen)

(Dr. Robert Stanford is sitting in his cabin looking at the files of the patients, there is a knock at the door, Dr. Robert Stanford looks up and then he says)

"Come in"

(Dr. John Hopes comes in to the cabin, and then he says)

"Chief you called me?"

"Yes, please sit down"

(Dr. John Hopes sits down on the chair opposite Dr. Robert Stanford, and then Dr. Robert Stanford says)

"You have heard about Joan Banks?"

"Yeah she banged into a glass door"

"Her mother wanted to sue the hospital and me?"

"Oh!"

"Now Dr. John Hopes you have to treat Joan Banks because Dr. Barry Johnson is no more? If they sue me then it is ok? But if they sue the hospital then name of our hospital will be tarnished?"

"Don't worry chief, I'll personally go and treat Joan Banks"

"Thank you, I just want her to leave this hospital as soon as possible"

"I understand chief"

(Dr. John Hopes gets up and then he goes and opens the cabin door and goes out)

(Helen, Rosalie, Dr. Anthony King, Wisdom and a janitor are standing in the hall of the reception counter, Amana is standing with her mother Samara and father Morale, Amana goes towards Helen, she gives a kiss on Helen's cheek and then she tells her)

"Thank you for everything and please Helen say goodbye to Mr. Mathews on my behalf? I'll be not able to face him and say goodbye?"

"I will and thank you also for being the best patient of this hospital"

(Amana hugs Helen and then she says)

"I'll always remember you?"

"I pray to god that you don't come to this hospital ever?"

"Thank you and god bless you?"

"God bless you to Amana"

(Amana then goes and hugs Rosalie, Dr. Anthony King, the janitor and then Wisdom, and then she says)

"First I did not wanted to come to this hospital, now I don't want to leave this hospital?"

(Tears fill the eyes of everyone, and then Wisdom tells Amana)

"I don't have a family but I would like you to call me elder brother?"

(Amana hugs Wisdom and then she says)

"You are a good-hearted person but you are also my forgetful brother?"

(Everyone laughs; Amana goes away with her mother and father, and then she turns and says)

"Helen you forgot to give me your magical hug?"

(Helen runs towards Amana and hugs her, and then she says)

"Now go please?"

(Amana goes away with her parents)

(Dr. John Hopes is opening the bandages from the wounds of Joan Banks, and then Dr. John Hopes puts fresh bandages from the tray that nurse Flora is holding in her hand, nurse Flora takes the old bandages of Joan Banks in the tray and goes out of the room, Dr.

John Hopes puts the last bandage on Joan Banks and then he asks her)

"How are you feeling?"

"A little pain is there in my head and the back of my body?"

"Which side of your head hurts?"

(Joan Banks shows the right side of her head. Dr. John Hopes touches the right side of the head and then he says)

"I think we will have to take an x-ray?"

"Ok doctor"

"Now show me your back?"

(Joan Banks turns and shows her back to Dr. John Hopes, Dr. John Hopes touches her back and then he tells her)

"I am moving my hand on your back now tell me where do you feel the pain?"

"Ok"

(Dr. John Hopes presses the back of Joan Banks backs below the neck, and then he asks her)

"Do you feel pain?"

"Yes"

(Dr. John Hopes then presses the back of Joan Banks further down and then he asks)

"Here also?"

"Yes"

"We will have to take an x- ray of your back also? Ok you can turn"

(Joan Banks turns and faces Dr. John Hopes, and then she says)

"I am having pain below my stomach wound also?"

(Dr. John Hopes pulls the dress of Joan Banks up, just beside the underwear of Joan Banks there is a black spot, Dr. John Hopes touches that black spot, Joan Banks shouts and holds Dr. John Hopes' hand with her hand)

"Ouch"

(Joan Banks hand is holding Dr. John hopes hand, he feels a electric shock run through his body, Joan Banks give a wicked smile, Dr. John Hopes has lost his way of thinking, Joan Banks holds the hand of Dr. John Hopes then makes him sit down beside her on the bed, Joan Banks gets up and takes Dr. John Hopes in her arms, Dr. John Hopes is so lost in his thought that he also puts his arms around the shoulder of Joan Banks, then Joan Banks presses her lips on Dr. John hopes lips, both are kissing each other, then after a few seconds Dr. John Hopes realizes what he is doing he gets up and then he says)

"I am sorry I got carried away?"

"I am also sorry"

(Then Dr. John Hopes turns and goes out of the room, Joan Banks smiles and then she says)

"This is the first nail in your coffin Dr. John Hopes"

(Tora Banks enters the room of Joan Banks, Joan Banks sees her mother, and then she smiles and says)

"Mom you missed a show"

"What show?"

"Dr. John Hopes and me hugging and kissing each other"

"You are fast my daughter?"

"As they say you want to do something tomorrow, do it today, and if you want to do it today, do it now?

"I knew that you would trap that son of a bitch"

"Just wait and watch mom, you are going to change your attitude from now onwards? Starting with Dr. Robert Stanford? Go give him a sweet talk of how you were wrong and blah, blah?"

"I want to break the head of that bastard"

"Forget that mom; just do what I tell you, ok?"

"Ok"

"Apologize to him, but don't try to seduce him because if you do then he will understand our game?"

"I am going to love it"

"Mom, when that wicked smile comes to your face I know that you are going to play your part well?"

"Yes just like old times when I used to fool men with my sweet talk"

"And be very careful that my dad does not know anything about this"

"Today he won't come because he has gone to the club"

"Ok mom, now get the fuck out of here?"

(Tora Banks turns and goes out of the room)

(Dr. Robert Stanford is making a round of the hospital; Dr. Robert Stanford comes in to the room of Mr. Mathews, Mr. Mathews is lying on the bed, Mr. Mathew's daughter-in-law Keith is sitting on the chair beside him, and then Dr. Robert Stanford asks Mr. Mathews)

"How are you today Mr. Mathews?"

"Fine chief"

"Very good, do you need anything?"

"No, thank you"

(Dr. Robert Stanford smiles at Keith and then he goes out of the room)

(Lauren Roy is lying on the bed, her husband Bill Roy is standing in front of her, and then Bill Roy tells Lauren Roy)

"Lauren, don't give me that talk that you won't be able to bare another child?"

"I am saying no more babies?"

(Dr. Robert Stanford comes in to the room and then he says)

"Hey Lauren how are you feeling today?"

(Lauren Rod looks angrily at her husband, and then she tells Dr. Robert Stanford)

"Bad, very bad"

(Dr. Robert Stanford smiling face turns serious, he asks Lauren Roy)

What is wrong with you?

"Nothing is wrong with me but everything is wrong with my husband"

(Dr. Turns and asks Bill Roy)

"Bill! What's wrong? I hope it is not about having more children's?"

(Tears comes into the eyes of Lauren Roy, and then she says)

"Yes that's what is wrong with him? He wants one more child?"

(Dr. Robert Stanford controls his anger, and then he tells bill Roy)

"Bill, we saved your wife from death and you want to risk your wife's life again?"

(Bill Roy says)

"But I love children?"

(Dr. Robert Stanford shakes his head, and then he tells Bill Roy)

"But you already have six children?"

"All of them are girls? I want a boy?"

(Dr. Robert Stanford is irritate, and then he asks Bill Roy)

"If the seventh one is again a girl then what will you do?"

"I'll try again?"

(Lauren Roy shouts)

"This man will kill me doctor?"

(Dr. Robert Stanford tries to reason with Bill Roy)

"Bill, see the health of your wife?"

(Bill Roy tells Dr. Robert Stanford)

"After she comes back home from the hospital? Then I'll have another child?"

(Lauren Roy is hysterical, She tells her husband)

"Bill you conceive one child, then you will know what trouble we women have to go through to bare a child?

(Dr. Robert Stanford tells Bill Roy)

"She is right"

(Bill Roy says)

"Without a son I have no respect in society?"

(Dr. Robert Stanford shakes his head and then he says)

"When a man talks without logic? I don't have an answer?"

(Dr. Robert Stanford goes out of the room, and then Lauren Roy tells her Husband)

"Look you motherfucker, when I come home and you even try to touch me I'll cut your balls off?"

"Screw you Lauren"

"Already you have screwed me and six daughters are born from it you bastard?"

(Dr. Robert Stanford comes in to his cabin. Tora Banks is sitting inside the cabin with two roses in her hand; Tora Banks gets up and then she says)

"Hello doctor?"

"Hello! Did you have any work with me?"

"Yes, first I want to apologize for my bad behavior, I am sorry?"

"That's ok"

"That is not ok, first tell you have forgiven me?"

(A smile comes on the face of Dr. Robert Stanford, and then he says)

"I respect people who realize their mistakes"

"Thank you, will you order a coffee for me?

"I will for sure?"

(Dr. Robert Stanford lifts the receiver of his phone and then he says)

"Please two coffees in my cabin"

(Then Dr. Robert Stanford puts the receiver down, and then Tora Banks says)

"Thank you doctor"

"Everyone calls me chief"

"Chief! Do I have to salute you before saying chief?"

"No"

(Tora Banks smiles, and then she says)

"Chief if you sit down on the chair then I can also sit down on the chair?"

"Oh?"

(Dr. Robert Stanford sits down on his chair, Tora Banks also sits down on the opposite chair, and then Dr. Robert Stanford says)

"You have a charming smile?"

"Oh thank you! I will tell you in my days I was an actor, men used to go crazy over my smile"

"You must have broken so many hearts in your days?"

"Like a coin has two sides, men and women are also like two sides of a coin, there was a man named Mick who broke my heart also?"

"Don't tell me?"

"Shall I show you his photograph?"

"Please?"

(Tora Banks takes out photographs from her purse, and then she goes towards Dr. Robert Stanford and then she tells him)

"See this photograph, this is Mick, and here is another photo of him"

(One by one Tora Banks shows the photographs to Dr. Robert Stanford, she gets very close to Dr. Robert Stanford, her boobs touching Dr. Robert Stanford right hand, Dr. Robert Stanford realizes this but does not move his hand, but Tora Banks remembers the words that her daughter had told her)

"But don't try to seduce him, because if you do then he will understand our game"

(Tora Banks goes back to her chair and sits down, Dr. Robert Stanford smiles and then he asks Tora Banks)

"But Tora I don't understand! Sometimes you are very sweet sometimes you are rude?"

"I was not like that before, but my husband troubled me so much that I have this sickness called insomnia"

"Insomnia! That's a very dangerous sickness, but you mentioned your husband troubles you?

(Tora Banks gets up and goes towards Dr. Robert Stanford, then she takes his right hand in her hands and then she says)

"First you have to promise me chief that whatever we say will remain between us, no third person should learn about our conversation?"

(Dr. Robert Stanford feels uproar in his body at the touch of tora banks hand, and then he says)

"I promise"

"You swear upon Doris?"

"I swear upon Doris"

"My husband is having an affair with a girl who is younger then my daughter"

"I don't believe it?"

"I knew you would say that, but truth is that this sickness of mine started after my husband got involved with this girl"

(Dr. Robert Stanford gets up from his seat and then he says)

"And I insulted you so much?"

"That's ok"

(Tora Banks brings tears to her eyes and hugs Dr. Robert Stanford, Dr. Robert Stanford puts his arms around Tora Banks, but again Tora Banks remembers the words of her daughter)

"But don't try to seduce him, because if you do then he will understand our game"

(Tora Banks again goes and sits down on the chair, and then Tora Banks says)

"That's why sometimes I become hard and sometimes I become soft"

"I really pity you"

"I understand your feelings chief, but I will tell you when I need your shoulder to cry on?"

"Oh! I wouldn't mind that?"

"I know that, now I will leave?"

(Tora banks gets up from the chair, and then Dr. Robert Stanford tells her)

"But your coffee is coming?"

"Chief you drink both the coffees? I will think that I have drank one coffee?"

"What a thought?"

"Please I will leave?"

(Dr. Robert Stanford gets up from his chair and then he goes and opens his cabin door, and then he tells her)

"It was a pleasure talking to you.

"The pleasure is all mine?"

(Tora banks go out of the cabin, and then Dr. Robert Stanford closes his cabin door)

(Joan Banks is having lunch, her mobile starts ringing, and Joan Banks looks at the number on the mobile and then she says to herself)

"That ass hole Tony? The stupid bastard will wreak my brains, but if I won't take his call he will come here?"

Joan Banks switches on her mobile and then she says)

"Yes Tony?"

(Joan Banks hears the voice of Tony)

"Hey Joan what's up"

"Please Tony I am really sick so don't call me again? I'll call you when I am ok?"

(Joan Banks switches off her mobile, Tora Banks comes in to the room, Joan Banks sees her mother 's face glowing, and then she asks her mother)

"Mom, I think you have scored a home run with Dr. Robert Stanford?"

"Yeah, I made him feel hot under his pants?"

"I hope you were in your limits?"

"I would have crossed my limit but your words, but don't try to seduce him, because if you do then he will understand our game stopped me"

(Joan Banks' normal face becomes vicious, and then she says angrily)

"After I take my revenge with Dr. John Hopes, you can use Dr. Robert Stanford as you want and kick his ass?"

"So what is my next move?"

"From now on, all the moves will be made by me, ok?"

"Ok"

(Joan Banks becomes normal, and then she smiles and asks)

"Now tell me, do you like Dr. Robert Stanford?"

"When he said, I pity you I wanted to spit on his face"

"Mom, it is so easy to fool a man?"

"Yeah, just make them a little hot under their pants and they will start dancing to your tunes"

"There are some tricks of the trade I have to learn from you?"

"In my time, even I did not know what I'd do next? Try to be wicked; then the wickedness comes from within you?"

"Mom, you are wicked"

"Thanks Joan"

"How did you get my innocent father to marry you?"

"If you don't mind, that secret will remain with me?"

"Ok!"

"Many men that we have jilted in our lives must be cursing us, calling us the vicious bitches?"

(Joan Banks and Tora Banks laugh, and then they hug each other)

(Helen and Rosalie are in their apartment watching TV, the phone bell rings; Helen picks up the receiver of the phone and then she says)

"Yes?"

(Jane is on the other line, and then she says)

"Helen it is me Jane"

(Helen tells Jane)

"Hey Jane what's up?"

(Jane says)

"I am at my mother's house in New Jersey"

(Helen tells Rosalie who is sitting beside her)

"Jane has taken Martha with her to New Jersey"

(Rosalie tells Helen)

"That's nice"

(Jane tells Helen on the phone)

"My mother, Mike and Martha are also with me"

(Helen tells Jane on the phone)

"You did a very good thing getting Martha away from New York? How is Martha?"

(Jane tells Helen)

"Martha is now getting back to normal, she is playing with our neighbor's children and their dogs, how is Rosalie?

(Helen says)

"You talk to Rosalie"

(Helen gives the receiver of the phone to Rosalie; Rosalie takes the receiver and then she says)

"Jane we really miss you?"

(Jane has tears in her eyes, she tells Rosalie)

"I also miss Helen and you"

(Rosalie tells Jane on the phone)

"Please take care of Martha?"

(Rosalie starts crying, Helen also has tears in her eyes, Rosalie gives the receiver of the phone to Helen and then she says)

"My voice is choking, you talk with Jane?"

(Helen takes the phone receiver from the hand of Rosalie, and then she tells Jane)

"Rosalie and I are going tomorrow to the beach with Dr. John Hopes and Dr. Anthony King"

(Jane tells Helen)

"Wow, please forget everything and enjoy yourselves?"

(Helen wipes her tears and then she tells Jane)

"We will, Jane we don't want to upset Martha so that's why we are trying to avoid talking to her?"

(Jane tells Helen)

"I understand Helen, don't worry, in a few days when Martha is ok, we all will go somewhere together?"

(Helen says)

"Like old times Jane?"

(Jane controls burst out crying, she tells Helen)

"Like old times Helen, I thing I'll go out and see Martha?"

(Helen tells Jane)

"Ok Jane take care and god bless"

"Jane says"

"God bless you and Rosalie"

(Helen puts the receiver down, and then she tells Rosalie)

"Rosalie, Jane told me that Martha is enjoying playing with the neighbor's children and their dogs?"

"It's a relief to hear that, but I really miss Martha?"

"I also miss Martha? What are you going to where tomorrow for the beach?"

"Bra and underwear"

"That's for the beach? What about the clothes?"

"We both should wear only bra and underwear, no clothes?"

"Why?"

"To make Anthony and John feel hot under their pants?"

(Helen and Rosalie both laugh and they hug each other)

(Jane is watching Martha play with neighbor's kids and their dogs, Martha makes an action with her hand telling Jane to come and play

with them, Jane gets up and then she goes and plays with Martha and the neighbor's kids, after a few minutes Jane tells Martha)

"Martha it is getting late let us go and have dinner?"

(Martha tells Jane)

"Jane you go and have dinner? This kids have invited me to their house to have dinner with them?"

(Jane smiles and then she says)

"Oh! Martha that's great?"

(Martha looks at the eyes of Jane, and then she asks her)

"Jane your eyes are full of tears? What is wrong?"

"Martha something has gone inside my eyes? I'll go inside the house and wash my eyes?"

"Ok?"

(Jane goes away inside the house; Martha starts playing with the kids and their dogs)

(It is eleven o'clock in the morning, the beach is full of people like young lovers, everyone is enjoying in the water, Helen and Dr. John Hopes, and Rosalie and Anthony King, come on the beach holding hands, Helen is wearing a beige colored swimsuit with flowers printed on it, Rosalie is wearing dark blue swimsuit with white colored boats printed on it, Dr. John Hopes and Anthony King are wearing colorful boxer shorts, they the lovers making love on the beach, and then Rosalie says)

"I think the beach is getting hotter and hotter?"

(Helen tells Rosalie)

"Just don't look at them?"

(Dr. John Hopes tells Helen)

"Helen let Rosalie look at the lovers? She is getting love making tips from them?"

(Dr. Anthony King says)

"John is right, we should learn some lovemaking tricks from these lovers?"

(All four laughs, then they go in to the water, for sometime they drown each other in the water, then Rosalie takes Helen on her shoulders and Anthony takes John on his shoulders, Helen and John fight with their hands to throw each other down in the water, John throws Helen and Martha in to the water, then they hug and kiss each other in the water, all four come out of the water and sit down on the sand, two couples come there, one man says to John)

"Do you two couple want to play switching couples with us?"

(Dr. John Hopes tells the man)

"We only switch livers from one patient to another?"

(The second man asks)

"What's that?"

(Dr. Anthony King tells the second man)

"We are doctors so we don't play switching partners?"

(The man tells Dr. Anthony King)

"Grow up?"

(Dr. John Hopes tells the man)

"You two are knocking on the wrong door?"

(Dr. Anthony King gets angry and tells the man)

"So buzz off"

(The two couples go away, and then Helen says)

"Let's go back to the hotel?"

(Rosalie smiles at Helen and then she says)

"Yes let's go?"

(They all get up and go towards the hotel)

(Dr. John Hopes and Helen are on the bed, they start making love, but Dr. John Hopes mind seems to be away, and then Helen asks Dr. John Hopes)

"What's wrong John?"

"I am just tired"

"Are you feeling ok?"

"Yeah I am ok, just a little headache"

(Helen starts pressing Dr. John Hope's head)

(Rosalie and Dr. Anthony King are on the bed in each other arms; Rosalie is trying to remove the boxer shorts of Dr. Anthony King, he holds on to his boxer shorts with his hands, and then he asks)

"Rosalie! What are you trying to do?"

(Rosalie smiles and then she says)

"I am removing your shorts so we can have sex?"

"Look Rosalie I have my reservations? So I won't have sex before Marriage?"

"Why?"

"If tomorrow suppose we are not able to marry then?"

"I am ready to take that risk and have sex with you?"

"No Rosalie? If our marriage does not come through then I don't want to have guilty conscious on my mind for the rest of my life?"

"Anthony we both are mature enough to have sex?"

"Rosalie I won't compromise with my principles?"

"But Anthony I am not able to control my feelings towards you?"

(Dr. Anthony King picks up Rosalie in his arms and then he takes her to the washroom and puts her down, then he opens the shower and says)

"Rosalie you will now cool down?"

(Rosalie hugs him, and then she says)

"Anthony at least let us make love in the shower?"

"Ok"

(Dr. Anthony King starts moving his hand all over the body of Rosalie)

(It is ten o'clock in the morning, at the reception counter of the Get-Well hospital Wisdom is writing on the work sheet, the phone bell rings, Wisdom picks up the receiver of the phone and then he says)

"This is Get-Well hospital and you are talking to Wisdom?"

(Helen comes there and picks up the work sheet, after listening to what someone is saying from the other side Wisdom says)

"Dr. Robert Stanford has still not come, can I take a message for him?"

(The other person cuts the connection, and then Wisdom looks at the receiver of the phone and says)

"At least say yes or no?"

(Wisdom puts the receiver down on the phone; and then Helen says)

"Good morning Wisdom"

"Good morning Helen"

"Your brain seems to be working very well today?"

"I had put hair oil in the night on my head?"

"I don't understand your logic?"

"Hair oil makes my blood run very well in my head?"

"Oh! I think you should put hair oil everyday in your head?"

"Everyday! Ok?"

(Helen smiles and goes away, and then wisdom tells himself)

"Because of the hair oil I have become a brainy man? So today I will buy a big bottle of hair oil and put the hair oil on my head everyday?"

(Joan Banks is looking very beautiful, she is sitting on the bed reading a religious book, Dr. John Hopes comes inside the room and then he says)

"Good morning to you Joan"

(Joan Banks looks up and then she says)

"Oh Dr. John hopes! Good morning"

"When we are alone you can call me John?"

"John! That means there is no formality between us?"

"That's right now let me check you?"

"Do I look ok today?"

"You look so beautiful today"

"Oh thank you so much"

(Dr. John Hopes checks Joan Banks with his stethoscope, when the hand of Dr. John Hopes goes on the chest of Joan Banks his mind stops working, Joan Banks realizes this, after a few seconds Joan Banks realizes that Dr. John Hopes is excited, and then she says)

"John I hope everything is ok?"

"What did you say?"

"I said John I hope everything is ok?"

"Yeah everything seems to be normal only your heartbeats are a little fast?"

"Come on John a handsome man like you touching me? My heart has to beat faster then normal?"

(Dr. John Hopes feels shy, and then Joan Banks says)

"Now stop being shy john?"

(Joan Banks takes Dr. John Hopes hand in her hands and kisses his hand and then she says)

"Sorry I could not resist it"

"You don't have to say sorry?"

"Ok I take back my words?"

"Thank you"

(Joan Banks sits up on her bed, and then she says)

"John after I get well and go from this hospital, I want you to have dinner with me at my house?"

"Sure!"

(Joan Banks hugs Dr. John Hopes and then she says)

"Oh I love you so much"

(Dr. John Hopes could not control himself and he also hugs Joan Banks and then he says)

"I love you too"

(For a few seconds Joan Banks and Dr. John Hopes remain in each other arms, and then Joan Banks says)

"I don't mind we remaining like this forever but John you have your reputation in this hospital?"

(Dr. John Hopes leaves Joan banks and then he says)

"Sorry I got carried away; you are worried about my reputation? I like that very much"

"Yes you are a respected doctor of this hospital and next time you come in to my room please lock the room from inside?"

"You really care for me Joan?"

"If I get a chance I'll prove to you that I can take care of you for a lifetime"

"Are you sure of what you said?"

"About me I am very sure, but I don't know about you?"

"You get better then we will sit and talk, ok?"

(Joan Banks gives that special smile of hers that has floored so many men in her life, and then she says)

"It is best if I go home, I will be suffocated in the hospital lying on this bed all day? John will you come to my house every day and attend to my wounds?"

"Yeah sure. I'll go and talk to the chief and explain your decision to him?"

"So sweet of you to do that for me"

"From now on, your wish is my command"

"I'll see to it that I always make you happy"

(Dr. John Hopes pats his hand on Joan Banks cheek and then he turns and walks out of the room, Joan banks wipe her cheek with her hand, and then she says)

"You bastard, I want to see you buried in a grave"

(Dr. Robert Stanford comes near the hospital reception counter, and then he tells Wisdom)

"Hey Wisdom, what's up?"

"Hey chief? What's up with you today?"

"Just fine"

(At that moment, Dr. John Hopes comes near the counter and then he tells Dr. Robert Stanford)

"Good morning chief, rather good afternoon?"

Dr. Robert Stanford smiles and then he tells Dr. John Hopes)

"Thanks for reminding me that it is the afternoon?"

(Dr. John Hopes and Dr. Robert Stanford both laugh, and then Dr. John Hopes ask Dr. Robert Stanford)

"Where were you all morning?"

"I was with my son Robert, we went to the store to buy household items"

"You have become a family man chief?"

"You are right john, Wisdom any calls for me?"

"A lady asked for you on the phone and I asked her if she wants to leave a message, but she disconnected the call?"

(Dr. Robert Stanford tells wisdom)

"I think she didn't like you?"

"But how could she see me on the phone?"

(Dr. Robert Stanford winks at Dr. John Hopes, and then he tells wisdom)

"She must have had a camera attached to her phone.

"I didn't know that! I hope you are not pulling my leg?"

(Dr. John Hopes laughs and then he tells Wisdom)

"Chief was pulling both your legs?"

(Dr. Robert Stanford, Dr. John Hopes and Wisdom laughs, and then Dr. John Hopes tells Dr. Robert Stanford)

"Chief, I want to talk to you?"

"Ok, but you will have to buy me coffee?"

"Yeah I'll buy you a coffee and you buy me a coffee? How's that?"

(Dr. Robert Stanford laughs, and then he puts his hand on Dr. John Hopes shoulders and then he tells him)

"I love your sense of humor John, let's go and have some fun with Bob?"

"Yeah, Bob is a soft nut to crack?"

(Dr. John Hopes and Dr. Robert Stanford turns and goes away from the reception counter, Wisdom smiles and then he says)

"If I had a clever brain then I would had been also a doctor in this hospital?"

(The two janitors Randy and David are sitting in the Get-Well hospital canteen having chocolate donuts; Bob comes and then he asks)

"I hope you liked my chocolate donuts?"

(Randy smiles, and then he tells Bob)

"They were just delicious"

(David finishes the last piece of chocolate donut, and then he tells bob)

"We have eaten donuts everywhere, but Bob no one can beat your donuts when it comes to taste"

(Bob says)

"Oh thank you so much, that will be four dollars"

(Randy asks)

"Hey Bob, we heard that you got married recently?"

"Yeah"

(David gets up from his chair and then he stretches his hand and then he tells Bob)

"Congratulations"

(Bob shakes the hand of David, and then he says)

"Thank you"

(Randy also gets up from his chair, and then he asks Bob)

"But where is the party?"

(Bob smiles, and then he says)

"Well, it was a court marriage?"

(David tells Bob)

"Oh! But you owe us one?"

"Ok, what do you two want?"

(Randy tells Bob)

"Instead of the party, just give us free coffee and donuts for a week?"

(David tells Bob)

"Bob what do you say?"

(Bob smiles and then he says)

"Ok, coffee and donuts on the house for you two for a week"

(Randy says)

"Let's go David"

(Randy and David go out of the canteen, Dr. Robert Stanford and Dr. John Hopes come in to the canteen, Bob sees them, and then he says)

"Chief and Dr. John Hopes! So nice to see you both?"

(Dr. Robert Stanford asks)

"Good afternoon Bob, I hope your donuts are ready?"

(Bob says)

"Yeah, they are"

(Dr. Robert Stanford says)

"Bob bring two chocolate donuts and two cups of coffee please?"

"Coming up chief"

(Bob goes away, Dr. Robert Stanford and Dr. John Hopes sits down on the chairs, and then Dr. Robert Stanford says)

"John, you wanted to talk to me?"

"Yes chief it is about Joan Banks, she wants to go home because she is getting suffocated in the hospital?"

"But her wounds haven't healed yet?"

"She asked me to go to her house and bandaged her wounds?"

"But the hospital will charge her for that?"

"I don't think she will mind?"

"Then it is ok, if Joan Banks is uncomfortable in the hospital, let her go to her house"

"Thanks chief"

"John, just treat Joan Banks wounds and not her heart?"

(Dr. John Hopes and Dr. Robert Stanford laughs, Bob brings two cups of coffee and two chocolate donuts on a tray, he puts the coffee and chocolates donuts on the table and then he says)

"Donuts and coffee"

(Dr. Robert Stanford looks at the eyes of Bob, and then he says)

"Bob, sit down"

(Bob sits down on the chair, and then Dr. Robert Stanford says)

"Bob, you seem very tired?"

(Bob looks at himself and then he says)

"I don't understand?"

(Dr. Robert Stanford and Dr. John Hopes start eating donuts, then they have a sip of coffee from the cup, Dr. Robert Stanford gives a serious look to Bob, and then he tells him)

"We want to talk to you about your sex life?"

"My sex life! What about it?"

(Dr. Robert Stanford puts both his hands below the eyelids of Bob, and then he says)

(Now a day you have to be very cautious about having sex with your partner"

"Chief you mean to say that I get Madeleine get checkup in the hospital?"

"No, no, I did not mean that"

"Then?"

(Dr. Robert Stanford looks at Dr. John Hopes, and then Dr. John Hopes tells Bob)

"It is very serious, listen to me carefully?"

"Yes Dr. John Hopes?"

"You are not having sex with your wife?"

"No?"

(Dr. John Hopes thinks for five seconds, and then he tells Bob)

"Let me think? You go and get two more chocolate donuts"

"Ok"

(Bob walks away towards his counter, Dr. Robert Stanford and Dr. John Hopes laugh, and then Dr. John hopes tells Dr. Robert Stanford)

"Bob has become quite serious?"

"We will give him some vitamin tablets and tell him to have one each day and give one to his wife each day, but that would be after we eat at least three donuts each?"

"Chief, you are really good at making a fool out of a person?"

"No, I am not good, I am very good?"

(Dr. Robert Stanford and Dr. John Hopes laugh, Bob comes with two chocolate donuts and puts it on the table and then he says)

"Dr. John Hopes and Dr. Robert Stanford, I am telling you something now but it must be a secret between the three of us?"

(Dr. Robert Stanford and Dr. John hopes say together)

"We swear by your donuts"

"I had promised you that I wouldn't have sex?"

(Dr. Robert Stanford is surprised, he then asks Bob)

"That means not even once did you had sex with Madeleine?

"No"

"Oh my god, you are doing everything wrong?"

"Oh!"

(Dr. Robert Stanford and Dr. John Hopes start eating the Donuts, and then Bob asks them)

"Please tell me what is wrong with me?"

(Dr. Robert Stanford looks Bob from the face down, and then he tells Bob)

"Everything is wrong, but don't worry we will give you tablet's, one tablet every day, you and your wife must take it before going to sleep.

"Why take tablets?"

"To keep your fly in good shape"

"Fly! What fly?"

"Bob you do the sex with a lady using what?"

"Oh!"

"Now we have to give you another advice, but please get two more chocolate donuts for us?"

"Oh sure"

(Bob gets up and goes away, and then Dr. Robert Stanford tells Dr. John Hopes)

"I was really confused that what do I tell him when he asked what is wrong with him?"

"Chief, Bob is an innocent guy, he will take any advice we give him?"

"That is right"

"Next time we come here to eat donuts, we will advice him to have oral sex?"

"Yeah that's a good idea?"

(Bob comes with two chocolate donuts and keeps it on the table, and then Dr. Robert Stanford asks Bob)

"We gave you such a good advice? Do we have to pay?"

"No. No, coffee and donuts are on the house"

"Bob come after one hour to my cabin and take the tablets from me?"

"Thank you"

"The pleasure is all ours, now go Bob, I and Dr. John Hopes have to decide what tablets to give you?"

"Ok"

(Bob goes away from the table, Dr. Robert Stanford and Dr. John Hopes look at each other and then they laugh)

(Tora Banks and Fred Banks are holding Joan Banks by the hand, as they enter their house, and then Joan Banks says)

"Home sweet home"

(Lily and Brandon are the servants of the house, Bowler and Cameron is the butler of the house, and James is the gardener of the house, all of them are standing inside the living room of the house, and then Lily says)

"So good to see you back ma'am Joan"

"Thank you Lily"

(Brandon bows down, and then he says)

"Welcome home ma'am"

"Brandon, I have heard that you and Lily are getting married?"

(Brandon smiles, and then he says)

"Only after you get married ma'am?"

"I like that, very soon your wish will come true, Bowler and Cameron what are you going to cook for me today?"

(Bowler tells Joan)

"Your favorite grilled chicken and chicken kebabs"

"Good, James is you taking care of my plants?"

(James tells Joan)

"They are in perfect shape ma'am"

(Joan looks at everyone, and then she says)

"I am going to rest, so don't disturb me?"

(Joan Banks by the support of her mother goes towards her bedroom, Joan's father goes away towards the staircase of the house and starts climbing the steps, then Joan and her mother go into the bedroom closing the door behind them, and then Lily says)

"Something is very wrong? I have never seen ma'am Joan in such a good mood?"

(Brandon says)

"I think the pain of the wound has kept ma'am Joan temper in control?"

(Bowler says)

"The house is so silent now? No one knows when the volcano will erupt?"

(Cameron says)

"I think some evil plan is developing in ma'am Joan's mind?"

(Brandon says)

"Joan madam's face looked like she was in a trance?"

(Lily says)

"Hope she doesn't loose her memory?

"Lily might be right? Let's cross our fingers and hope that lily's wish come true?"

(Bowler says)

"No, no, nothing has happened to her, she was supposed to stay in the hospital for ten more days? She is planning something; and the sky is going to fall on us very soon?"

(James says)

"Yeah this is impossible? How can a witch turned into Cinderella?"

(Everyone laughs)

(Joan Banks is sitting on the bed, Tora Banks is sitting on the sofa beside her bed, and then Joan Banks tells her mother)

"Mom, from now on you have to be very good with the house staff"

"Ok"

"Keep your hatred and anger in control?"

"Ok, I'll be nice to the staff"

"Until Dr. John Hopes and I get married?"

"Oh!"

"And I also want you to be very loving towards my father in front of Dr. John Hopes?"

"Ok, But?"

"Any problem?"

"First promise me you won't be angry?"

"Ok, I promise"

"I told Dr. Robert Stanford that your father is having an affair with a young girl from his club?"

"Why did you say that?"

"To attain sympathy from Dr. Robert Stanford"

"Mom, in the future, doesn't make a scrape goat of my father?"

"Sorry it was a slip of the tongue"

"As much as I love you, I love my father also?"

"I said sorry?"

(Joan Banks dials a number on her mobile, she then tells her mother to go away by waving her hand, and then Tora Banks gets up from the sofa and goes out of the bedroom)

(Dr. John Hopes is studying a case in his cabin, his mobile rings, Dr. John Hopes switches on his mobile and puts the mobile on his ear and says)

"Dr. John Hopes?"

(On the other end, Joan banks who has called Dr. John Hopes says)

"Hello John, this is Joan"

(Dr. John Hopes hears the voice Joan on his mobile, he gets so excited that the mobile almost falls down from his hand, and then Dr. John Hopes says)

"Hello Joan"

(Joan Banks knows from the voice of Dr. John Hopes that he is nervous, and then Joan says)

"I just called to say that I got home"

(Dr. John Hopes is so nervous that he says)

"Yes, yes"

(Joan Banks smiles and then she says)

"I hope I didn't disturb you"

(Dr. John Hopes takes a deep breath and controls himself and then he says)

"No, no, I was sitting idle; it is a pleasure to be talking to you"

(Joan Banks laughs and then she says)

"The pleasure is all mine, John, I was wondering if you could come and see me tonight"

(Dr. John Hopes heart starts beating faster, he controls his voice and then he says)

"Oh sure, is there anything I can get for you in the evening?"

(Joan Banks says in a sexy tone)

"I just want you John?"

(These words of Joan Banks get Dr. John Hopes so excited that he says)

"I'll be there at eight thirty sharp?"

(Then Joan Banks says in a loving voice)

"How am I going to pass my time up until eight thirty?"

(Now Dr. John Hopes is really anxious to meet Joan Banks, so he says)

"Do you want me to come earlier than eight thirty?"

(Joan says)

"Make it at eight o'clock"

(Dr. John Hopes holds his mobile tight and then he says)

"Ok, ok, I'll be there at eight o' clock?"

(Joan says)

"Ok see you"

(Joan Banks switches off her mobile)

(Dr. John Hopes says)

"Hello, hello? Oh the connection must have cut off?"

(Dr. John Hopes hangs up; there is a knock on the door, and then Dr. John Hopes say)

"Come in"

(From the door Helen comes in, and then she says)

"Hi John?"

"Helen! You?"

"Sorry! Have I disturbed you?"

"It's ok; I was just going through a patient reports"

"Well, I wanted to ask you if we are going out tonight?"

"Tonight! Where?"

"We decided to go to the restaurant?"

"No, no, not tonight"

"Why, is there any urgent work?"

"Yeah, I have work pending in the hospital?"

"Oh! Something is wrong with you?"

"Nothing is wrong?"

"You seem different today?"

"These reports are disturbing, that's all?"

"Ok, some other time, see you?"

"Yeah see you"

(Dr. John Hopes goes on looking at the reports, Helen gives him a look for five seconds, then she goes out of the door, and then Dr. John Hopes looks at the door and says)

"Oh god, what do I do? Helen is my life but I am in love with Joan?"

(Rosalie is sitting on the sofa watching TV, a scene is playing on the TV, a man tells his wife)

"I know you are everything to me but?"

(The wife asks her husband)

"But what?"

(The man says)

"I am confused"

(The wife says)

"Confused! Why?"

(There is a commercial break on the TV)

(Helen comes in the apartment, Rosalie sees Helen, and then she says)

"Hi Helen"

"Hi Rosalie"

(Helen comes and sits beside Rosalie on the sofa; commercial break on the T.V. is over, the scene between the man and the wife is playing on the TV, the man tells his wife)

"I know I still love you, but I also love my secretary?"

(The wife tells her husband)

"You can't do that! Either you choose me or your secretary?"

(Tears come in to the eyes of the man, and then he says)

"I can't live without you? And I can't live without my secretary?"

(The wife is angry, and then she says)

"Suppose we are at the sea and there is a storm, I am in one boat and your secretary is in another boat, now you have one foot in my boat and the other foot in your secretary's boat, how will you be able to sail both boats? Either you take your foot out from your secretary's boat and come in to my boat or take your foot out of my boat and go in to your secretary's boat?"

(The man takes his wife in to his arms, and then he says)

"What would you do if you were in my place?'

(The wife takes her husband's hands in her hands, and then she says)

"I would never let this kind of a situation come in my life?"

(The man again puts his arms around his wife's neck, and then he says)

"Won't you give me a few days?"

(The wife smiles, and then she says).

"No, you are a man, take your decision right now?"

(The episode ends on the T.V. And then Rosalie asks Helen)

"Helen, what decision do you think the husband will take next week? Will he stay with his wife or go away with the secretary?"

"I think I can give you the answer before the week is over?"

"Come on Helen, you have always made decisions for others? I am making coffee for both of us; I want the answer after I make the coffee?"

"Ok"

(Rosalie goes away, Helen takes out her mobile and dials a number, then she hears that the mobile is switched off, she switches off her mobile, and then she dials another number on her mobile, and then she says)

"Sharon I am Helen, is Dr. John Hopes still in his cabin? What! Ok, thank you"

(Helen switches off her mobile, Helen then looks up, and then she says)

"Is my life story coming to a standstill?"

(Rosalie comes with two cups of coffee, she gives one cup to Helen, and then she asks)

"Did you think of the answer?"

"Yes, the husband will leave the wife and go away with the secretary"

"That was very quick! How did you guess the answer?"

"You can say sixth sense"

"Oh! Hey Helen you were going to go out with Dr. John Hopes in the night, right?"

"I think that Dr. John Hopes may not be interested in going out with me?"

"What are you saying Helen?"

"We decided to go a restaurant tonight but Dr. John Hopes told me he is busy in the hospital, but right now I called him and he did not pick up his mobile, then I called the hospital and Sharon told me he went away after I left the hospital"

"But why would Dr. John Hopes lie to you?"

"He must have his own reasons?"

"Better talk to him tomorrow?"

"Look Rosalie, I don't want to create a scene?"

"You want me to talk to him?

"No Rosalie, it is his life let him decide what he wants? Come on; let's go for a movie?"

"Ok, but first let's go and eat a burger at burger king?"

"That's a good idea, let's go?"

(Helen and Rosalie open the door and go out of the door, and then they close the door behind them)

(There is a doorbell at Joan Banks house, the house servant Lily opens the door, Dr. John Hopes is standing outside the house with flowers and a gift in his hands, and then Lily asks him)

"Yes?"

"I am Dr. John Hopes from the Get-Well hospital, Joan Banks is expecting me"

"Oh yes, please come in"

(Dr. John Hopes enters the house, Lily closes the door, and then lily tells Dr. John Hopes)

"Please come?"

(Dr. John Hopes walks behind Lily, they come near the bedroom door, and then lily points to the door and tells him)

"You can go in Doctor"

"Thank you"

"You are welcome Doctor"

(Lily goes away, Dr. John Hopes knocks on the door, and from inside the bedroom Joan Banks says)

"Come in"

(Dr. John Hopes opens the door and goes in, and then he closes the door behind him)

(Joan Banks is sitting on her bed reading a book, Joan Banks is wearing a beige colored short dress, she has a little makeup on her face, she is looking stunning, Dr. John Hopes goes near her, admires her beauty, Joan Banks closes her book, then she Looks at Dr. John hopes and then she says)

"Welcome to my house John"

Thank you Joan, this is for you"

(Dr. John Hopes gives the flowers and the gift to Joan Banks, Joan Banks takes the flowers and the gift and then she says)

"Flowers! I love flowers. What's in the wrapping?"

"Open it and see for yourself?"

(Joan Banks smiles, then she opens the gift, inside the wrapping paper there is a box of chocolates, a perfume, a big purse and a sweater, and then Joan Banks says)

"Wow! What beautiful gifts?"

"Beautiful gifts for a beautiful woman"

(Joan Banks gives a hug to Dr. John Hopes, and then she says)

"I will never forget this day in my life"

"I didn't know that you would be so happy with the gifts! Next time I'll bring two gifts for you?"

"Oh! I'll reward you now for these gifts"

"My pleasure"

(Joan Banks kisses Dr. John Hopes on his lips for two minutes, and then Joan Banks asks)

"I hope you liked your reward?"

"I loved it and I'll repay you right now"

(Dr. John Hopes kisses Joan Banks on her lips, Joan Banks swings Dr. John Hopes on to her bed, then kissing each other Joan Banks presses her body against Dr. John Hopes body, they continue kissing and caressing each other, after five minutes Joan Banks separates herself from Dr. John hopes and then she says)

"Let's go and eat dinner"

"Ok"

(Dr. John Hopes gets up and goes with Joan Banks towards the door, Joan Banks opens the bedroom door, and then they both go out of the bedroom door)

(Lily and Brandon are standing near the dining table, Joan Banks and Dr. John Hopes comes near the dining table, Joan Banks points to a chair and then she tells Dr. John Hopes)

"John you sit here"

(Dr. John Hopes tells Joan Banks)

"Thank you"

(Dr. John Hopes sits down on the chair, Joan Banks goes and sits down on the chair opposite to Dr. John Hopes, and then Joan banks tells Lily)

"Tell Bowler and Cameron to bring the food"

"Yes ma'am"

(Lily goes away, and then Joan Banks tells Dr. John Hopes)

"I have told my butler's to make chicken kebabs and grilled chicken, because they are my favorite dishes"

"I love grilled chicken and chicken kebabs"

"Oh! Our choice of food is the same?"

(Bowler comes with two trays of grilled chicken and chicken kebabs, he then puts both the trays in front of Dr. John Hopes, Cameron also comes with two trays of grilled chicken and chicken kebabs, he then puts both the trays in front of Joan Banks, Lily comes with a jug of water and two glasses and puts it down on the table, and then Joan Banks tells her staff)

"You can all go now"

(Everyone goes away, and then Joan Banks tells Dr. John Hopes)

"I like to drink water with food"

"That's a good habit"

"Well, you can serve yourself, I hope you don't mind?"

"Not at all"

(Dr. John Hopes takes grilled chicken, then chicken kebabs and starts eating, Joan Banks also takes grilled chicken and chicken kebabs and starts eating, and then Joan Banks asks Dr. John Hopes)

"How is the food?"

"It is so delicious? That I think I will have to come again and again to your house?"

That's nice, you will be coming in to check me so I'll tell my butler to prepare only grilled food for you"

"And when you get better, what will I do then?"

"My home is your home and I am not letting you go off so easy?"

"Oh! So now my dinner problem is solved?"

"Everyday, there will be a different grilled item like grilled fish, and grilled mutton kebabs?"

"And what are you going to give me for dessert?"

"Five kisses, five hugs and five love making positions"

"Kisses and hugs I can understand? But what are five love making positions?"

(Joan Banks gives one of her smiles that no man can resist the temptation to take her in his arms, and then Joan banks says)

"You better finish the food because it is going cold"

"Your smile has made my stomach full?"

"That's a nice compliment?"

"Thank you, oh by the way I don't see your parents?"

"They have gone to a party, not to the same party, but to the different parties"

"I think that your mother and father are not getting along well with each other?"

"Every family has their own problem but they love each other that is why they are together?"

"I am sorry I should not have said something about your mother and father?"

"You don't have to apologize John, whenever we are together we will only talk about ourselves?"

"Ok, what are your future plans?"

"Do you believe in destiny?"

"Yes?"

"Then leave everything to destiny"

"Ok"

"After food I always drink red wine, hope you will give me company?"

"Sure"

"Now let's finish our food?"

(Joan Banks and Dr. John Hopes go on eating their food)

(Helen is in the lobby of a movie theatre, Rosalie is standing beside her eating popcorn, Helen dials a number on her mobile, and then she waits for sometime and switches off her mobile, and then Rosalie asks Helen)

"Were you dialing Dr. John Hopes' number?"

"Yes, but the mobile is switched off?"

"Do we go to the house of Dr. John Hopes from here?"

"No he might be sleeping"

(Joan Banks pours wine in two glasses, her back is towards Dr. John Hopes who is sitting on the bed in Joan's bedroom, Joan Banks puts a small brown color tablet inside one glass of wine, then Joan banks gives that glass which has the tablet inside it to Dr. John Hopes, and then she says)

"Cheers"

(Dr. John Hopes touches the glass of Joan banks and then he says)

"Cheers"

(Then they both drink their wine from the glass, Dr. John Hopes finish off the wine from his glass and again pours some wine inside his glass, Joan Banks finish her wine, and then she say)

"I drink only one glass of wine, if you want you can have as much as you want?"

(Dr. John Hopes finishes his glass of wine and then he says)

"I had enough"

(Joan Banks takes Dr. John Hopes in her arms and starts kissing him, they both start making love on the bed)

(Helen is sitting on the sofa of her apartment; Rosalie comes there, and then she tells her)

"Shall we go to sleep?"

"I don't feel like sleeping?"

"You want me to give you company?"

"No, you go to sleep, I'll join you after sometime"

"Ok, good night"

"Good night"

(Rosalie goes away, Helen gets up and paces back and for in the living room, she again dials a number on her mobile, then waits for a few seconds, then Helen switches off her mobile, and then she says to herself)

"First time in my life I am feeling unsecured?"

(Helen again goes towards the sofa, and then sits down on the sofa, she is so frustrated that she again gets up and starts pacing around, and then she says)

"I think Dr. John Hopes is in trouble?"

(Dr. John Hopes is sleeping on the bed of Joan Banks, Joan Banks is sleeping beside him, both are nude, only a bed sheet is covering them, Dr. John Hopes opens his eyes, he looks at himself and then towards Joan Banks, he is so shocked to see that he is nude and even Joan Banks is nude, he touches Joan Banks, Joan Banks yawns and then opens her eyes, and then she says)

"Good morning John"

"Joan, how did this happen?"

(Joan Banks gets up and sits on the bed, and then she says)

"You came so strong on me that I could not control you?"

"Oh my god!"

"It is ok John, you and I are old enough to have sex with each other?"

"I am really sorry Joan?"

"When I have no complaints against you, why are you feeling sorry?"

"Thank you Joan, you are being very kind to me"

"When two people get involved with each other and there is love and trust between them? Sex is a normal thing?"

"I am serious about you Joan, but I don't know what is my place in your heart?"

(Joan Banks holds Dr. John Hopes in her arms, and then she says)

"If I had not been serious about you John, I would not have let you touch me?"

"Oh!"

"From today onwards don't try to double cross me?"

(Dr. John Hopes kisses Joan Banks on her lips, and then he asks)

"And what would you do if I double cross you?"

"I'll make your face such a mess that no other woman will even look at you?"

(Dr. John hopes smiles, and then he says)

"I get your message? But I love you more than you love me?"

"That I will know only after we marry?"

"Do you want to marry so fast?"

"Not so fast, but we have to think about it?"

"When you are ready to marry, tell me?"

(Joan Banks and Dr. John Hopes starts making love)

(Wisdom is sitting at the reception counter of the hospital, he has a bruise on his left cheek, he is holding a ice bag to his left cheek nursing the bruise, Helen comes there and looks at Wisdom, and then she asks him)

"Now how did you get that bruise?"

"My girlfriend gave it to me"

(Helen laughs, and then she asks wisdom)

"Your girlfriend! Why?"

"She had called me day before yesterday to her house to meet her parents; I forgot and went yesterday to her house and she gave me one punch on my cheek"

"Oh! Wisdom you should not have forgotten to go day before yesterday?"

"You know Helen my brain stops working sometimes"

"Did you say sorry to her?"

"For saying sorry, she gave me the second punch"

"For saying sorry she gave you the second punch! Why?"

"When I went the next day she gave me the first punch, I asked her why did she hit me, she told me that she and her parents were waiting for me yesterday so I said sorry and she gave me the second punch so that I don't make the same mistake again?"

"Oh! Ok tell me why did you call me?"

"One second"

(Wisdom looks at a paper, and then tells her)

"Dr. John Hopes had called for you to help him with a patient in the outpatient clinic"

"Thank you"

(Helen turns then she stops and turns again, and then she tells Wisdom)

"Next time your girlfriend tells you something, write it down on a piece of paper like you wrote it now?"

"Yes from now on I am going to carry a pen and a paper in my pocket"

"You are getting clever day by day?"

"Thank you"

(Helen laughs, and then she turns and goes away)

(Dr. John Hopes is cleaning a wound of a patient who is lying on the bed, the patient is young boy who is twenty years old, the boy is Caucasian, he is wearing jeans and a white t-shirt, and he is very handsome, his hair is brown, he looks from a decent family, the boy's left hand is handcuffed to the bed, Dr. John Hopes is cleaning his wound, Helen comes there, and then she says)

"Good morning Dr. John Hopes"

"Good morning to you Helen"

"Why is this boy's left hand handcuffed to the bed?"

"He is a thief"

(Helen lifts the tray, which is lying on the bed, and then Helen asks the boy)

"What did you steal?"

"Food from a store"

"In America you get so many benefits from the government and still you steal?"

"It was just for fun but I regret my mistake"

"You should. Dr. John Hopes, is it serious?"

"No, just a scratch"

"Last night I called you so many times, your mobile was switched off? Where were you?"

"Last night my old friend called me and we went for drinks, in the morning I found that my mobile battery was dead"

"When I asked you to go out with me you said that you had some work in the hospital?"

"My friend had come from Canada and he was leaving again for Canada by morning flight?"

(Helen looks at Dr. John Hopes and Dr. John Hopes takes his eyes away, and then Helen tells the boy)

"So mister thief repeats what I say?"

(Instead of looking at the thief Helen looks at Dr. John Hopes. Dr. John Hopes is surprised that Helen is looking at him and not at the boy, and then Helen says)

"From today onwards I won't commit any crime"

"From today onwards I won't commit any crime"

"From today onwards I'll never lie to anyone"

"From today onwards I'll never lie to anyone"

"From today onwards I'll never be dishonest"

"From today onwards I'll never be dishonest"

(A police officer wearing his uniform comes in to the room with a man, the man is an Indian, he is forty years of age, the man is wearing a white pant and a white shirt, black hair, round face, and then the police officer asks Dr. John Hopes)

"Doctor can I take him away?"

"Just give me five minutes?"

"Ok"

(Helen tells the police officer)

"Officer, this boy is so young, if you put him in jail his full life will be spoiled, can't you forgive him on humanity grounds?"

"Ma'am, I understand what you are trying to say, but I can't do anything; this man is the owner of the shop from where this boy has stole the food?"

(Helen tells the man who is an Indian)

"Sir, please I request you not to press charges on this young boy, once the thief stamp is on the boy then everybody will disrespect him? Just think that he is like your son?"

(The man looks at the boy who has tears in his eyes, and then the man tells the Police Officer)

"Officer, I like to withdraw my complain against this boy?"

"Ok, but still the boy has to come to the police station, he has to give in writing an apology letter?"

"Thank you so much officer"

(Helen extends her hand towards the Indian man, and then she tells the man)

"I appreciate it, sir"

(The man shakes the hand of Helen, and then he says)

"Women like you have made America the best country in the world?"

(Helen bows her head, and then she says)

"Thank you"

(The police officer opens the handcuff from the bed, and then the boy tells Helen)

"Ma'am only thing I can say is god bless you"

"God bless you to"

(The police officer takes the boy away, the man also goes away with the police officer, and then Dr. John Hopes tells Helen)

"What a wonderful thing you did Helen?"

"Thank you"

"You were telling the boy not to lie, not to be dishonest, but you were looking at me as if you were trying to make me understand those words?"

"Yes I wanted you to understand those words"

"Do you mean to say that what I told you about my friend from Canada is all lies?"

"Yes"

(Dr. John Hopes gets angry, and then he shouts at Helen)

"You are telling me that I am a liar?"

"Yes"

"You have no right to say that?"

"Why my right over you is over?"

"We had agreed that for one year we wouldn't interfere in each other lives?"

"Oh! So you want to do whatever you do and you want me to keep quiet also?"

"But what have I done?"

"Your face is not supporting your words?"

"Because I am shocked that you are doubting me?"

"Your lies have also shocked me?"

"You are talking nonsense today"

(Helen shouts)

"I am not talking nonsense, I am talking sense"

"I am not committed to you to give you clarification for my day-to-day plans?"

"Ok! Now that you made it clear that I am nothing to you? We should finish off our relationship?'

"I don't mind?"

"If you go to see, what you wanted to tell me I have said it, right?"

"You can think any way you like I don't care"

"Dr. John Hopes you don't care for me that is already written on your face, I just wanted to hear it from your mouth"

"It is senseless to argue with you anymore"

(Dr. John Hopes leaves the clinic, and then Helen says to herself)

"I think I will have to face the truth that everything is over between Dr. John Hopes and me; my love life chapter is closed"

(Tears rolls down the cheek of Helen, she sits down on the bed, and then she starts crying)

(Dr. Robert Stanford is looking at the reports of a woman named Barbara who is sitting opposite him in his cabin, and then Dr. Robert Stanford tells Barbara)

"Barbara your report says that you have to be operated upon?"

"Oh!"

"Don't worry it is a minor operation?"

"Ok"

"When do you want to go for the operation?"

"Tomorrow if it is possible?"

"I think I have to talk to my doctors? So I will talk to them and call you on your mobile?

(Barbara gets up and extends her hand, and then she says)

"Fine, I'll be waiting for your call?"

(Dr. Robert Stanford shakes hands with Barbara, and then he says)

"Ok and take care Barbara"

"You too doctor"

(Barbara turns and goes out of the cabin; Dr. Robert Stanford dials a number on his mobile, and then he says)

"Dr. John Hopes can you come to my cabin for five minutes? Thank you"

(Dr. Robert Stanford switches off his mobile, Dr. Robert Stanford gets up and stretches his arms; there is a knock on the door, and then Dr. Robert Stanford says)

"Come in"

(Dr. John Hopes comes inside the cabin, Dr. Robert Stanford sees Dr. John Hopes and then he says)

"Hello John"

"Hello chief"

"Can you do an operation tomorrow for a kidney stone?"

"Sorry chief, but I am not feeling well so I was actually going to come to you to tell you that I want to rest for a day or two?"

"No problem, I'll tell Dr. Anthony King to do the operation? But you seem very upset?"

(There is a knock on the door, and then Dr. Robert Stanford says)

"Come in"

(Rosalie comes in to the cabin; her eyes are filled with tears, and then she tells Dr. John Hopes)

"Dr. John Hopes you have no right to treat Helen so badly?"

"Look Rosalie this is a personal matter between Helen and me?"

"That's what I am trying to tell you? Why do you want to break personal relationship with Helen?"

(Dr. Robert Stanford gets up from his seat, and then he says)

"One second Rosalie, Dr. John Hopes what has happened between you and Helen?"

(Dr. John Hopes says)

"Helen wanted to finish off our relationship and I said ok?"

"But why would Helen wants to cut off relation with you John?"

"You better ask her?"

(Rosalie tells Dr. Robert Stanford)

"I just came from out patient's room and Helen was sitting on the bed crying. I asked her what is the matter and she said that Dr. John Hopes is lying to her about last night?"

(Dr. Robert Stanford says)

"But Helen asked me about you Dr. John Hopes in the morning, she wanted to know about last night and I told her that you had gone to Joan Banks house to check her?"

(Hearing this Dr. John Hopes walks out of the cabin, and then Rosalie tells Dr. Robert Stanford)

"And all the time Dr. John Hopes was lying to Helen that he had gone for drinks last night with his old friend?"

"Oh!"

(Rosalie starts crying, and then she says)

"Chief, almost the full night Helen was calling Dr. John Hopes worried about something has happened to him and he had switched off his mobile"

"I understand what you are saying but Rosalie this a personal and private matter of Dr. John Hopes, nobody can interfere?"

"Dr. John Hopes has broken Helen's heart, he will never be happy in his life?"

(Rosalie goes out running from the cabin, and then Dr. Robert Stanford says)

"I hope Dr. John Hopes is not digging his own grave?"

(Doris opens her eyes, nurse Jennings is sitting beside her, Jennings is thirty-five years of age, about five feet two inches tall, round face, brown eyes, brown hair, Jennings gives a smile to Doris, and then Doris asks Jennings)

"What is your name?"

"Jennings"

"Your first name?"

"Teri"

"Teri Jennings?"

"Yes"

"You are new here?"

"Yes, I just joined the hospital few days back, before that I was working for downtown hospital"

"Oh! The same hospital that Wisdom came from?"

"Yes, but I am not as forgetful as Wisdom?"

(Doris smiles, and then she asks Jennings)

"Can you please call the chief?"

"Ok"

(Jennings picks up the receiver of the intercom phone lying on the small table, then she dials one zero one, and then she says)

"Chief, Doris is conscious and she wants to talk to you, so will you please come to her room? Ok, thank you"

(Jennings puts the receiver back on the phone, and then she tells Doris)

"Chief is coming"

"Thank you, can I ask you why did you leave the downtown hospital?"

(Jennings smiling face becomes grim; she looks at Doris for a few seconds, and then she says)

"In a car accident I lost my husband, my seven-year old son and my five-year-old daughter, so I left that place and came here so that I can forget the tragedy that happened in my life?"

"I am sorry, I did not know about your tragedy, I am really sorry?"

"No problem, only thing I regret is that why did I not go with my family to the market on that day when this accident happened?"

(Dr. Robert Stanford comes in to the room, Jennings gets up, and then she tells Doris)

"Excuse me"

(Jennings goes out of the room, Dr. Robert Stanford comes and sits on the chair beside Doris, and then he asks her)

"How are you feeling Doris?"

"After hearing the story of Teri Jennings I think my pain is nothing compared to her pain?"

"Yes I know, but she is a very brave woman"

"She did not shed a single tear when she told me of her tragedy?"

"She knows how to face the reality of life?"

"Yeah you are right? So how are you chief?

"Fine, I am only waiting for the day I can take you to my house?"

"What will be the first thing you do when you take me to your house?"

"Send our son Robert to live with my friends"

(Doris laughs, and then she asks)

"Are you thinking of bringing another member into our family?"

"Yes, I love daughters?"

"And suppose another son is born?"

"I'll go on trying until I get a daughter?"

"Oh! Can I suggest something?"

"Go on, I am listening?"

"There are so many children who don't have parents, why don't we adopt a girl?"

"That's a wonderful idea Doris?"

"Thank you"

(Dr. Robert Stanford mobile starts ringing, Dr. Robert Stanford switches on his mobile, and then he puts the mobile on his ear and says)

"Yes?"

(Then Dr. Robert Stanford hears the voice from the other side, and then he says)

"Ok, I am coming"

(Dr. Robert Stanford switches off his mobile, and then he tells Doris)

"I have to go?"

"Ok"

"I love you"

"I love you too"

(Dr. Robert Stanford turns and goes out of the room of Doris)

(There is a doorbell at the house of Joan Banks, Lily the Servant opens the door, Dr. John Hopes is standing outside the House, Lily sees Dr. John Hopes, and then she says)

"Please come in doctor?"

(Dr. John Hopes comes inside the house, and then Dr. John Hopes asks Lily)

"Ma'am Joan is there in her bedroom?"

"Ma'am is having a face massage, please sit down on the sofa"

(Dr. John Hopes sits down on the sofa, and then Lily asks him)

"What can I get you?"

"Coffee please"

"Yes sir"

(Lily goes away, Dr. John Hopes lifts a magazine from the center table and turns the pages, Tora Banks comes in to the Living room, and she sees Dr. John Hopes and then she says)

"Hello Dr. John Hopes"

(Dr. John Hopes sees Tora banks and gets up, and then he says)

"Hello ma'am"

"Please sit down"

(Dr. John Hopes sits down on the sofa, Tora Banks sits down on the sofa opposite Dr. John hopes, and then she says)

"It is so good to see you doctor, thanks for taking care of Joan?"

"It is a pleasure to treat Joan, ma'am"

"Joan was talking a lot about you, what a good-hearted person you
    are"

"So nice of Joan to say that"

"I was very nasty with you in the hospital, so please forgive me"

"It is ok ma'am"

(Tora banks dials a number on her mobile, and then she says)

"Joan, Dr. John Hopes is waiting for you in the living room, ok?"

(Tora banks switches off her mobile, and then she tells Dr. John Hopes)

"Doctor, Joan has called you in to the bedroom"

(Dr. John hopes gets up, and then he says)

"Thank you and bye"

"Bye doctor"

(Dr. John Hopes goes away from the hall towards the bedroom of Joan Banks; he opens the door and goes inside the bedroom)

(Inside the bedroom Joan Banks is combing her hair, she has worn a short yellow colored dress, Dr. John Hopes goes towards her, and then he says)

"Hello Joan"

(Joan Banks goes on combing her, and then she says)

"Hello john, wonderful to see you, please sit down I'll be with you in a minute"

(A lady who was giving massage to Joan Banks picks up her vanity case and goes out of the bedroom, and then Dr. John Hopes says)

"You are looking very beautiful today"

"After you have come in to my life, I want to look the best"

"Your beauty is really captivating"

(Joan Banks smiles and goes towards Dr. John Hopes, and then she sits down beside Dr. John Hopes, and then she says)

"What about you John? Your blue eyes are reminding me of a beautiful blue colored sea, you are so handsome that I want to hold your face and make love to you day and night?"

"The pleasure will be all mine"

(Joan Banks lightly kisses Dr. John Hopes on both cheeks, she kisses his forehead, chin, nose, neck, and then she takes Dr. John Hopes in her arms and holds him for one minute with moving her fingers through his hair, the mobile phone of Joan Banks rings, Joan Banks leaves Dr. John Hopes, and then she says)

"Excuse me"

"Ok"

(Joan Banks gets up and goes towards a table where her mobile phone is lying, Dr. John Hopes admires Joan Banks from the back and smiles, he then gets up and follow Joan Banks, Joan Banks lifts her mobile, and then she switches on the mobile phone and then she says)

"Yes mom?"

(Dr. John Hopes puts his arms around Joan Banks from the back, Joan Banks says on the mobile)

"Tomorrow? Ok? Thank you mom, I love you"

(Joan Banks turns around and faces Dr. John Hopes, she puts both her hands around Dr. John hopes' neck, and then she says)

"John, how would you like to get married to me tomorrow?"

"What!"

"Surprised?"

"More than surprised?"

"So what is your answer?"

"I hope you are not pulling my leg?"

"No I am serious?"

"But the preparation of the wedding?"

"I will sign on a court paper and you will sign on a court paper, that's it"

"Oh! But what about going to church and the priest getting us married?"

"That will have to wait, my four new movies are going on the sets, if the producer comes to know about my marriage then I'll be thrown out of all of the four movies"

"Ok, I understand, but I am sharing an apartment with Dr. Anthony King?"

"After marriage you will stay at my house"

(Dr. John Hopes starts thinking, and then Joan Banks asks him)

"Any problem?"

"No, I think it is a good idea for me to stay here with you?"

"I knew you would like it, everyday in the evening you can come here from the hospital and go to the hospital in the morning from here?"

"But your mom won't mind me staying here?"

"Mom was the one who gave me this idea of you staying here with me after the marriage"

"Your mom is a darling?"

(Joan Banks smiles and takes Dr. John Hopes in her arms, and then they start kissing each other)

(Helen and Rosalie are having dinner at their apartment, and then Rosalie tells Helen)

"Helen, shall we both take leave for two days and go to Jane's house in New Jersey?"

"Look Rosalie there is shortage of nurses in our hospital, nurse Flora is on leave? Nurse Sally is also on leave?"

"Oh! I forgot"

"And the chief will also have a tough time adjusting the nurses in the hospital"

(The door bell rings, and then Helen tells Rosalie)

"I'll open the door"

(Helen goes and opens the door, Dr. Anthony King is standing outside the door, Helen smiles and then tells him)

"Dr. Anthony King! Please come in?"

"Thank you Helen"

(Dr. Anthony King comes inside the apartment, Helen closes the door, and Rosalie looks at Dr. Anthony King, and then smiles and says)

"Anthony! So nice to see you?"

(Dr. Anthony King sits down on the chair of the dining table; Helen also sits down and then she asks Dr. Anthony King)

"Will you have dinner?"

"No, thank you"

(Rosalie looks at the grim face of Dr. Anthony King, and then Rosalie asks Dr. Anthony King)

"You seem very serious! Is everything ok?

(Dr. Anthony King takes out an envelope from his pocket and gives it to Rosalie, Rosalie takes the envelope, and then takes out a letter from the envelope and starts reading the letter, Helen looks at Dr. Anthony King and then at Rosalie reading the letter, Dr. Anthony King Pours water in a glass from a jug lying on the dining table, then Dr. Anthony King slowly drinks the water from the glass, Rosalie finishes reading the letter, then she gives the letter and the envelope back to Dr. Anthony King Rosalie looks shocked so Helen asks Rosalie)

"What is it Rosalie?"

"Dr. Anthony King has got a marriage proposal for his four sisters from a man from Africa, the man wants to marry his four sons to Dr. Anthony King's sisters, but he wants Dr. Anthony King to marry his only daughter first and stay forever-in Africa"

"Oh!"

(Dr. Anthony King finishes drinking the glass of water, and then he asks Rosalie)

"Rosalie what is your decision?"

"Look Anthony, you will never get this kind of opportunity in your life, my advice to you is go to Africa and get married to that girl, because it is a question of the life of your four sisters?"

"But Rosalie?"

"Look Anthony I always wanted you to be happy, so don't have any second thoughts?"

(There is silence for ten seconds, and then Rosalie tells Dr. Anthony King)

"And once you go to Africa and get married, I don't want you to write me letters or call me?"

"Why?"

"I don't want any trouble in your married life?"

(Dr. Anthony King gets up and goes out of the apartment closing the door behind him, and then Rosalie tells Helen)

"The food is getting cold, let's eat?"

(Rosalie and Helen eat their food in silence)

(It is morning Dr. Robert Stanford is in his cabin writing the reports in his file, there is a knock on his door, and then Dr. Robert Stanford says)

"Come in"

(Dr. Anthony King comes in to the cabin of Dr. Robert Stanford, and then he says)

"Good morning chief"

(Dr. Robert Stanford without looking up says)

"Good morning Dr. Anthony King, please sit down?"

(Dr. Anthony King sits on the chair opposite Dr. Robert Stanford, and then he says)

"Chief, this kidney stone operation is the last operation I will be doing?"

(Dr. Robert Stanford is shocked; he looks up towards Dr. Anthony King, and then he asks)

"What do you mean by this operation is your last operation?"

"I am leaving America and going to Africa?"

"What?"

'Chief I am sorry to leave this hospital with out proper notice"

(Dr. Robert Stanford's surprised face turns to anger, he gets up and goes towards Dr. Anthony King, and then he asks him)

"Will you please explain it in detail?"

(Dr. Anthony King takes out the envelope and gives it to Dr. Robert Stanford, and then he tells him)

"You better read it yourself?"

(Dr. Robert Stanford snatches the envelope from Dr. Anthony King hand, he then takes out the letter from the envelope and starts reading it, Dr. Anthony King mobile phone rings, he takes out his mobile from his pocket and switches on the mobile, and then he says)

"Yes?"

(Then he hears the voice from the other side, and then Dr. Anthony King says)

"Yes Dr. Bill Conrad keep everything ready for the operation, I'll be in the operation theatre in just ten minutes, thank you?"

(Dr. Anthony King switches off his mobile phone and puts the mobile phone in his pocket; Dr. Robert Stanford gives the envelope and the Letter to Dr. Anthony King, then he goes and sits down on his chair and asks))

"Dr. Anthony King what about Rosalie?"

"I had a talk with her last night in her apartment and she said that I should go to Africa"

"Well, after reading this letter the only thing I can say is best of luck"

"Thank you chief"

Dr. Robert Stanford eyes are wet with tears; he turns his back on Dr. Anthony King, and then he says)

"Please go"

(Dr. Anthony King looks at the back of Dr. Robert Stanford for a few seconds, and then he turns and goes out of the door of the cabin)

(The person from the court, Mr. Robin Rivers is sitting opposite Joan Banks and Dr. John Hopes, Joan's mother Tora Banks and father Fred Banks are standing behind Joan Banks and Dr. John Hopes, there are two court papers in front of Joan Banks and Dr. John Hopes, and then Mr. Robin Rivers tells Joan Banks and Dr. John hopes)

"Please both of you sign both the papers?"

(Joan Banks signs the first paper and then she signs the second paper, Dr. John Hopes signs the first paper and then the second paper, and then Robin Rivers tells Tora Banks and Fred Banks)

"Please, now you both sign the papers below as witnesses?"

(Tora Banks signs both the papers, and then Fred Banks signs both the papers, Robin Rivers smiles, and then he tells Joan Banks and Dr. John Hopes)

"Now you are both man and wife"

(Joan Banks and Dr. John Hopes get up and shake hands with Robin Rivers, Robin Rivers takes both the papers, and then he says)

"I will take both the papers and complete the formalities of the court, after fifteen days you will receive one of these papers by mail"

(Mr. Robin Rivers bows his head then turns and goes away, Tora Banks hugs Joan Banks and Dr. John Hopes, and then Fred Banks hugs Joan Banks and Dr. John Hopes, and then Tora banks tells Fred banks)

"Let's go"

(Tora Banks and Fred Banks go towards the staircase of the house and start climbing the staircase, and then Joan Banks tells Dr. John hopes)

"Congratulations, my husband"

"Congratulations, my wife"

(Then they both kiss each other on the lips, and then Dr. John Hopes asks Joan Banks)

"I don't see the servants, the butlers, and the gardener of this house?"

"I have given all of them leave today"

"Leave today! Why?"

"The news of us getting married would be disaster for my acting career, so I sent them on leave"

"Oh!"

"We are wasting time on these stupid talks, let us go and enjoy our married life in the bedroom?"

(Dr. John hopes smiles and lifts Joan Banks in his arms and carries her towards the bedroom, then Joan Banks opens the bedroom door with her hand and then they both go inside the bedroom)

(Dr. John Hopes comes in to the bedroom carrying Joan Banks in his arms, Dr. John Hopes puts Joan down on the bed, and then Joan Banks tells Dr. John Hopes)

"From Joan Banks now I have become Joan Hopes but in people's eyes I'll remain Joan Banks, ok?"

"Ok"

(Joan Banks takes Dr. John Hopes in her arms, and then they start making love)

(Tora banks is touching up her face with make-up in the bedroom, Fred Banks is pacing left to right and right to left, and then Tora Banks tells Fred Banks)

"Why are you getting hyper?"

(Fred Banks stops moving, and then he says)

"I have never understood you in my life? Now I don't understand Joan also?"

"Look Fred she wanted to get married just for fun"

"Marring for fun? I am disgusted?"

"My daughter's wish is my command, I'll go to any limit to see my daughter happy"

"Dr. John Hopes is a respected doctor and our daughter is playing with his feelings?"

"My daughter and I are actors, the only feelings we show are on the screen, ok?"

"But coping with our daughter won't be easy for Dr. John Hopes, he might hurt her?"

"If Dr. John Hopes touches my daughter then he is dead man"

"Please Tora there is still time, put some sense in your daughter's head, otherwise it will be too late and you will repent the rest of your life"

"I don't know how I married a weak man like you?"

"I should say that why I married a witch like you?"

"Witch! Me?"

"Yes you"

"One day I will show you what limit I will go to destroy you"

"You have already destroyed my self-respect, I am just a servant to you"

"One day I will see that I make you my pimp"

"Pimp?"

(Fred Banks gets angry and moves towards Tora Banks, Tora Banks takes out a revolve from her purse, and then she says)

"In this gun, there are six bullets and I really want to pump in to you all six of them?"

(Fred banks look at the gun and stops, and then Tora Banks says)

"Show me that you are a real man?"

(Fred Banks knows that his wife is looking for a chance to shoot him, so Fred Banks waits for her to lower her gun, Tora Banks has that wicked smile on her face that Fred Banks knows is a deadly smile, Fred Banks turns around and goes out of the bedroom, Tora Banks grits her teeth, and then she says)

"Someday, I am going to shoot you, you bastard"

(Joan Banks is getting dressed, she is in her bra and panties, she puts on a dress from above her head, the dress is a violet colored with printed black flowers, she then wears violet colored four inch heel shoes, her hairs are open, and she has a light violet colored lipstick on her lips. Dr. John Hopes comes out of the washroom in a towel wrapped around his waist, Dr. John Hopes looks at Joan Banks, and then he asks her)

"Are we going out?"

"No"

"Then why are you dressed up?"

"I am going to a party"

"I can't come with you?"

"No"

"Why not?"

"Because you are not invited"

"You can't just go and leave me alone in the house?"

"Slowly, you will get used to it"

"I'll get used to it! You mean to say that you won't take me with you to any party of yours?"

"I had made it clear to you that in public eyes I am single?"

"But one day you will have to let the public know that we are married?"

"When the right time comes, I will announce it in public"

"And when will that right time come?"

"I don't know"

"Come on Joan I am your husband? Don't confuse me?"

(All of a sudden, Joan Banks gets wild and takes the lamp from the table and throws it down on the floor, the lamp breaks and the glass gets shattered all around, Joan Banks looks angrily at Dr. John Hopes, and then she points her finger towards him and says)

"Don't fuck with me you motherfucker?"

(Dr. John Hopes is so taken a back by Joan's language that he just sits down on the bed and goes on looking at Joan Banks, and then Joan banks says angrily)

"If you want then you can take your things and get the fuck out of here?"

(Tora Banks opens the bedroom door and enters the bedroom, and then she goes towards her daughter and asks)

"Why are you so angry Joan?"

(Joan Banks points at Dr. John Hopes, and then she tells her mother)

"This motherfucker is getting on my nerves"

(Tora Banks pats Joan Banks on the back, and then she tells Joan Banks)

"Ok, you go, I'll get things straight?"

(Joan Banks lifts her violet purse from the table and walks out of the bedroom door closing the door with a bang, and then Tora banks tells Dr. John Hopes)

"What is your problem?"

"I just asked Joan to take me to the party with her?"

"Who are you to ask that?"

"I am her husband?"

"Listen to me carefully Dr. John Hopes? My daughter's private life is her own life? Don't try to interfere in her private life ever in the future, this time she has broken the Lamp on the floor, the next time she will break it on your head"

(Dr. John Hopes is so shocked that continues staring at Tora Banks, and then Tora Banks tells Dr. John Hopes)

"And would you mind putting some clothes on?"

(Dr. John Hopes gets up and goes inside the washroom, closing the door behind him, Tora Banks looks at the shattered glass on the floor, and then she says)

"I have never lifted a vessel in my life! How am I going to lift this glass?"

(Tora Banks sits down on the bed, and then she says)

"All the servants are also on a leave?"

(Dr. John Hopes comes from the washroom door inside the bedroom wearing a black pant and black shirt, and then Tora banks tells Dr. John Hopes)

"Dr. John Hopes, please clear this shattered glass from the floor before Joan comes back"

"Me?"

"If you want to live here, you have to do some work?"

(Tora Banks goes out of the bedroom closing the door behind her, Dr. John Hopes sits down on the bed and then he says)

"I think I have burnt my fingers getting married to Joan?"

(Dr. John Hopes takes paper napkins from the table and starts picking up the glass pieces)

(Helen and Rosalie are having dinner on the sofa, Rosalie switches on the T.V, and an emotional scene is going on between a husband and a wife, the husband holds his wife's hands in his hands, and then he says)

"Look Carolyn I said I am sorry."

(The wife is very angry; she takes out her hand from the husband's hands, and then she tells him)

"Adam, you betrayed me by having an affair with your secretary?"

"Please Carolyn, forget the past and think about the future."

"Honesty is such a sacred thing between a husband and a wife and cheating on your wife is an unforgivable offence."

"Carolyn you should give me one more chance?"

"Adam, for six months, the mental torture I have gone through has made me a strong woman, now I will decide what is right for me and what is wrong for me?"

"I beg you to give me one more chance."

"If I ask you a question, swear upon god that you will you give me an honest answer?"

"I swear upon god"

"Instead of you, if I had betrayed you and slept with another man, would you have taken me back as your wife?"

"No"

"Well, you have got your answer?"

(The wife takes her suitcase and walks out of the door, closing the door behind her)

(Helen smiles, and then she tells Rosalie)

"The story on the TV resembles my own personal life?"

"Yeah, you can say that again?"

(The main door opens, from the door, Jane and Martha come inside the house, Jane smiles and then she says)

"Hello?"

(Helen and Rosalie are so happy to see Jane and Martha, they both run and hug Jane, and then Helen and Rosalie hug Martha, and then Martha says)

"I really missed you?"

(Helen says)

"It is a pleasant surprise to see you both?"

(Martha says)

"I and Jane thought of giving you both a surprise?"

(Rosalie says)

"And we loved your surprise?"

(They all sit down on the sofa, and then Jane says)

"I am really hungry?"

(Helen says)

"So join us?"

(Jane and Martha eat from Helen and Martha's plate, Helen looks at Jane and then she asks her)

"Jane, something is on your mind. What is it?"

(Jane smiles, and then she says)

"You really read my thoughts Helen?"

(Helen smiles back, and then she says)

"You know me?"

(Jane stops smiling, and then she says)

"We heard about you and Dr. John Hopes and about Rosalie and Dr. Anthony King?"

(Helen has a sad smile on her face, and then she says)

"Well, to make a long story short, it is all over for us?"

(Martha says)

"You two could have called us?"

(Rosalie says)

"Helen and me didn't want to upset you two?"

(Jane says)

"I know that you both love Martha and me more than yourself, but then what are friends for?"

(Helen says)

Helen—Rosalie and I wanted to come to New Jersey to meet both of you, but the problem was that the hospital is short of nurses?"

(Jane says)

"Oh?"

(Rosalie says)

"There is shortage of Doctors and nurses in the hospital?"

(Martha says)

"We already know that? The chief told us?"

(Helen says)

"Oh! So the chief also told you our stories?"

(Jane says)

"Yeah, you know the chief was crying on the phone like a baby?"

(Helen says)

"He is a good man, he treats the hospital staff like his own family"

(Jane says)

"Helen, I am like your sister and I don't want to hide anything from you about Dr. John Hopes"

(Helen tells Jane)

"You want to tell me that Dr. John hopes is staying with Joan Banks?"

(Jane says)

"Yeah and?"

(Helen tells Jane)

"Look Jane, if you tell me anything about Dr. John Hopes, it won't make any difference to me?"

(Jane says)

"The chief had a talk with Dr. John Hopes and the way Dr. John Hopes talked to the chief, the chief thinks that Dr. John Hopes has married Joan Banks?"

(Helen smiles, and then she says)

"If he has done that, then I pity him?"

(Jane gets angry, and then she says)

"Pity him! Are you out of your mind?"

(Helen tells Jane)

"Jane, marring a woman like Joan Banks is like a man committing suicide?"

(Angrily Jane gets up, and then she says)

"I don't understand you Helen?"

(Helen also gets up, and then she faces Jane and says)

"I am just being practical in life?"

(Tears comes out of the eyes of Jane, and then she holds Helen in her arms and says)

"I really admire your guts Helen?"

(Tears comes out of the eyes of Helen, and then she tells Jane)

"The good times and the bad times should both be taken positively? Ok, now let's talk about ourselves?"

(Rosalie gets up, and then she says)

"Let us forget everything and play cards after we eat the food?"

(Helen smiles, and then she says)

"As they say, unlucky in love but lucky in cards?"

(Everyone laughs)

(Dr. John Hopes is sitting in Joan Banks bedroom, he looks at his watch and then he says)

"It is one' o clock and Joan has still not come?"

(Then Dr. John hopes goes near the window of the bedroom, a car comes and stops outside the house, a man gets down from the car and opens the other door of the car, Joan Banks gets down from the car half drunk, the man helps Joan Banks reach the main door of the house, the man goes away to his car and drives off, and then Joan Banks opens the main door with the key, Dr. John Hopes says)

"Oh my god! She is drunk?"

(Dr. John Hopes moves towards the bed and stands near it, Joan Banks open the bedroom door and comes in, and then Dr. John Hopes says)

"Joan, it is one's clock in the night?"

"So what do I do? Dance for you?"

"And you are dead drunk?"

"So what?

"And I also saw an unknown man drops you home?"

"That unknown man is my old boyfriend?"

"Old boyfriend?"

"Yes, he picked me up from the house and dropped me home, so what's the big deal?"

"Let's eat dinner?"

"I already ate at the party, now don't bug me and let me sleep?"

(Joan Banks throws her shoes from her feet and goes and sleeps on the bed; Dr. John Hopes just goes on looking at her)

(It is morning, Helen, Rosalie, Martha and Jane are at the hospital reception, Helen and Rosalie are in the nurse uniform, Jane and Martha are in their casual wear, Wisdom who is behind the counter looks at them, and then he says)

"So nice to see all four of you together?"

(Jane says)

"We four are friends so we will be always together? But Wisdom you don't have any boyfriend?

(Wisdom has a shocked expression on his face, and then he says)

"Boyfriend! I am not gay?"

(Everyone laughs, and then Jane tells Wisdom)

"Sorry, my mistake Wisdom. It was a slip of the tongue?"

(Wisdom says)

"Jane, your tongue will encourage men and pull them towards me thinking that I am an easy prey for them?"

(Everyone laughs, and then Helen says)

"Wisdom looks neutral?"

(Wisdom asks Helen)

"Neutral! That means half man and half what?"

(Everyone laughs again; Helen catches both her ears with her hands and then she tells Wisdom)

"We were just testing you to see whether or not you were okay?"

(Wisdom asks)

"Am I a car that you were testing me?"

(Rosalie says)

"Now you are a hundred percent ok Wisdom?"

(Wisdom laughs and claps his hands, and then he says)

"I was just playing with you, I know you all four love me so much, you all are so good hearted that you can never hurt anyone in life?"

(Martha says)

"Wisdom, you are out standing! Let me give you a hug?"

(Martha gives a hug to Wisdom, and then Martha leaves wisdom and asks him)

"How was the hug?"

(Wisdom tells Martha)

"I think I want one more hug?"

(Martha gives another hug to Wisdom, and then she leaves Wisdom and asks him)

"Are you happy?"

(Wisdom tells Martha)

"Only if you give me two hugs every morning?"

(Martha smiles, and then she asks Wisdom)

"Why two hugs every morning?"

(Wisdom becomes shy, and then he tells Martha)

"After you gave me two hugs, my heart started beating like the strings of a guitar?"

(Martha says)

"Oh! Wisdom you are a clever person?"

(Wisdom says)

"No? I am a human?"

(Everyone laughs, Dr. John Hopes comes there, and then he says)

"Hi everyone?"

(Everybody turns his or her face away; Helen looks at Dr. John Hopes, and then she says)

"Hi Dr. John Hopes"

(Dr. John Hopes asks)

"Helen, can I talk to in private for five minutes?

(Helen asks Dr. John Hopes)

"Why in private?"

(Dr. John Hopes tells Helen)

"It is personal, so please?"

(Rosalie wants to say something but Jane says no to Rosalie by performing a no gesture with her head, and then Helen tells Dr. John Hopes)

"What do you want to say that you got married to Joan Banks?"

(Dr. John Hopes is shocked to know that Helen knows that he is married to Joan Banks, and then Dr. John Hopes says)

"I can explain?"

(Helen tells Dr. John Hopes)

"From today, there is no personal relationship between you and me, only professional?"

(Dr. John Hopes looks at everybody and then he goes away, and then Wisdom says)

"I have never hurt a fly in my life, but today I wanted to beat up Dr. John Hopes?"

(Everyone is surprised and looks at Wisdom, Helen extends her hand and then she tells Wisdom)

"Thank you Wisdom"

(Wisdom shakes hands with Helen, and then he says)

"Helen, remember that you have a brother here?"

(Tears comes in to the eyes of Helen, and then she says)

"Brother?"

(Wisdom points everyone, and then he says)

"But remember? I am only Helen's brother?"

(Everyone laughs, then Wisdom comes out from behind the counter and wipes the tears of Helen from her eyes with his hands, Helen takes both the hands of wisdom in her hands and kisses them, and then Helen says)

"Now that Wisdom has made me his sister, Rosalie and Martha what do you think of him?"

(Rosalie looks Wisdom from head to toe, and then she says)

"He is too simple and you know we are too out going?"

"The way I talk? Did you find me simple?"

(Martha tells Wisdom)

"Rosalie meant that loving a person and adoring a person is quite different?"

(Wisdom puts his hand on his throat and swears, and then he says)

"If I want? I can even make a butterfly fall in love with me?"

(Everyone laughs, and then Jane says)

"But butterflies and humans have a vast difference between them?"

(Wisdom says)

"But both have hearts?"

(Rosalie smiles, and then she says)

"Suppose I think of marring you? What will you do for me?"

(Wisdom says)

"I will carry you in my arms from your house to the church?"

(Rosalie is shy, and then she says)

"So sweet of you! Thank you?"

(Wisdom tells Rosalie)

"Only thank you?"

(Rosalie is surprised, and then she asks Wisdom)

"What more do you want?"

(Wisdom bends down on his knees, and then he extends his hand and tells Rosalie)

"Your hand in marriage?"

(Rosalie looks at everyone, they all say yes by shaking there heads in a yes gesture, Rosalie smiles, and then she says)

"I need a little time to think about it?"

(Wisdom extends his other hand, and then he tells Rosalie)

"I will wait for you for a lifetime?"

(Rosalie feels shy, and then she says)

"I think I need a coffee break?"

(Wisdom gets up, and then he holds Rosalie with his hand and says)

"Do you want me to get it for you?"

(Rosalie says)

"No"

(Rosalie goes away running from there, and then Jane tells Wisdom)

"Wisdom you are the first person who has made Rosalie blush?"

(Wisdom with both his hands holds himself, and then he says)

"Well I think I am a romantic at heart?"

(Helen asks Wisdom)

"But Wisdom, what will happen to your girlfriend if you marry Rosalie?"

(Wisdom puts his head down, and then he says sadly)

"She patched up with her old boyfriend and got married to him? But I am a strong-hearted man?"

(Helen, Jane and Martha say together)

"We think so too"

(Then Helen, Jane and Martha go away from there, Wisdom is so happy that he dances and goes behind the counter, and then while dancing Wisdom tells himself)

"I didn't know I was so handsome! I will buy a small mirror tomorrow and see my own face every minute of the day"

(A boy is brought on the stretcher; an iron rod has gone in to the body of the boy, the iron rod has pierce the body of the boy from the stomach and has come out two inches from the back, the boy is conscious, the boy's mother is there with him, four hospital janitors are pushing the stretcher towards the operation theatre, outside the operation theatre Dr.

John Hopes, nurse Helen, nurse Rosalie come running, Dr. Bill Conrad is a newly appointed Doctor comes running there, Dr. Bill Conrad is a Caucasian, he is six feet two inches tall, handsome face, strong built, brown eyes, and then the mother of the boy tells Dr. John Hopes and Dr. Bill Conrad)

"Please doctors save my son, I have no one besides him?"

(Dr. Bill Conrad puts his hand on the shoulder of the woman who is the boy's mother, and then he tells her)

"Ma'am, we will save your son, the good news is that he is still conscious, that means that the iron rod has made no serious damage to the organs of your son's body?"

(The janitors take the boy inside the operation theatre, Dr. John Hopes, Dr. Bill Conrad, nurse Helen, nurse Rosalie go inside the operation theatre and close the door of the operation theatre)

(Inside the operation theatre, one doctor is already there, Dr. John Hopes, Dr. Bill Conrad, Helen and Rosalie comes into the operation theatre, and then Dr. Bill Conrad says to the doctor)

"Doctor, give him the anesthesia injection?"

(The doctor gives the boy the anesthesia injection, and then Dr. John Hopes tells the boy)

"Look, we are going to pull the rod from the front; you will have to be very brave?"

(The boy has tears in his eyes, and then he says)

"I have my mother's blessing with me? Do what you want with me? But please save me?"

"Nothing is going to happen to you?"

"Thank you"

(Dr. John Hopes looks at Dr. Bill Conrad, and then he asks)

"Doctor, do we start?"

"Yes Dr. John Hopes, now all of you hold the boy tightly, when we pull the rod, the boy should not shake?"

(Dr. John Hopes and Dr. Bill Conrad hold the rod from the front, the four janitors, nurse Helen, nurse Rosalie hold the boy tightly, Dr. John Hopes and Dr. Bill Conrad pulls the rod from the boy's stomach, the boy is in pain but does not say anything, the rod is taken out, and then the blood comes out of the boy's body)

(Outside the operation theatre, the boy's mother is sitting on the bench and praying, the mother's relatives are sitting on the bench with her, some of the relatives are standing)

(Inside the operation theatre, Dr. John Hopes and Dr. Bill Conrad are operating on the boy, Dr. John Hopes is sweating and nurse Helen wipes the sweat of off Dr. John Hopes' face, and then Dr. Bill Conrad asks Dr. John Hopes)

"Doctor, are you ok?"

(Dr. John Hopes says in a tired tone)

"Yeah, I am ok"

(Nurse Helen continues wiping the sweat off of Dr. John Hopes' face)

(Outside the operation theatre, the boy's mother is sitting with her relatives; one of the relative brings a cup of tea, and then she tells her)

"Grace, it's been six hours and you haven't eaten anything? So please drink this tea?"

"Thank you"

(Grace takes the cup of tea and starts drinking, Helen comes out of the operation theatre, on seeing Helen, grace stands up and then she ask her)

"Nurse, how is my son?"

"The rod has been taken out and the operation is a success, your son is just fine"

"Oh! Thank you nurse?"

"Thank the lord"

(Helen turns and starts walking, Grace and the relatives look up and start praying)

(Helen and Rosalie are sitting in the hospital canteen, Helen is drinking coffee from a mug, and then Helen asks Rosalie)

"Are you sure you don't want to have tea or coffee?"

"No Helen, I am good"

(At that time Dr. Bill Conrad comes near the table where Helen and Rosalie are sitting, and then Dr. bill Conrad says)

"Good evening to you two?"

(Helen smiles, and then she says)

"Good evening Doctor"

(Dr. Bill Conrad says)

"May I ask that what was wrong with Dr. John Hopes when he was in the operation theatre?"

(Rosalie says in an irritating tone)

"Dr. Bill Conrad now what personal problem Dr. John Hopes has in his life? We don't know anything about it?"

(Dr. Bill Conrad says)

"I just asked because Dr. John Hopes' hand was shaking all the time in the operation theatre?"

(Rosalie again says in an irritating tone)

"Doctor your question can be answered only by Dr. John Hopes? So you better ask him when he comes to the hospital tomorrow morning?"

(Dr. Bill Conrad smiles, and then he says)

"Ok? And good night?"

(Helen says)

"Good night Doctor"

(Dr. Bill Conrad turns and goes away, Helen smiles, and then she asks Rosalie)

"Rosalie you are irritated? Why?"

"I don't want anybody to take the name of Dr. John Hopes in front of me?"

"I know you care for me so much Rosalie? But just forget the Dr. John Hopes and my episode?"

(Rosalie gets angry, she gets up from her chair and then she tells Helen)

"How can I forget that Dr. John Hopes ditched you and left you in the lurch? If I had my way I would have spit on the face of Dr. John Hopes?"

(Rosalie starts crying, Helen gets up from her chair and takes Rosalie in her arms, and then Helen tells Rosalie)

"Let's go home Rosalie?"

(Helen holds Rosalie in her arms and goes out of the hospital canteen, Bob who was watching the scene looks up, and then he says)

"God if you are up there watching then don't ever forgive Dr. John Hopes for his sins"

(Dr. John Hopes rings the bell of Joan's Banks house, the servant of the house Lily opens the door and then she says)

"Hello doctor"

"Hello Lily"

(Dr. John Hopes comes inside the house, Lily closes the door, and then Dr. John Hopes asks Lily)

"Where is Joan Ma'am?"

"She is inside the bedroom with an old friend, but she has given strict instruction not to let anybody inside the bedroom?"

(Dr. John Hopes is angry, and then he says)

"What the hell?"

(Dr. John Hopes moves towards the bedroom, Lily follows him, and then she says)

"Doctor please don't go inside the bedroom?"

(Dr. John Hopes opens the door of the bedroom, Joan Banks is sitting on the bed, her old boyfriend is lying on the bed with his head on Joan Banks lap, and then Dr. John Hopes asks Joan Banks)

"Joan! What is this?"

(Joan Banks tells Dr. John Hopes)

"My old boyfriend had a fight with his girlfriend, so he has come here to ask for my advice"

"Your old friend is taking advice from you by putting his head on your lap?"

(The old boyfriend gets up, and then he says)

"Who are you to ask this question to Joan?"

(Dr. John Hopes tells Joan Banks)

"Joan, why don't you tell this man who I am? Or do you want me to tell him who I am?"

(Joan tells her old boyfriend)

"You better go?"

(Joan Banks old boyfriend goes out of the bedroom closing the door behind him, and then Joan Banks asks Dr. John Hopes)

"Did Lily not stop you from coming inside my bedroom?"

"Yes, she did?"

"Oh! So you disobeyed my order?"

"I am not your servant? I am your husband?

"Who says so?"

"I say so?"

"What evidence do you have that you are my husband?"

"You don't remember the court paper we both signed?"

"The paper is still not registered in the court?"

"Oh! Thank you for telling me this?"

Joan Banks gives a wicked smile to Dr. John Hopes, and then she says)

"But I can still prove that you are my husband if I want? But you can't prove that I am your wife?"

"You are trying to blackmail me! Ok, right now I am walking out of your house and your life?"

(Dr. John Hopes goes out of the bedroom, Joan Banks follows him, Dr. John hopes opens the main door of the house and goes outside towards his car, Joan Banks follows him, Dr. John Hopes opens his car door and sits inside it, Joan Banks opens the other door and sits inside the car, and then Dr. John Hopes tells Joan)

"Please get out of my car?"

"You can't walk out of my life without my permission?"

"Who the fucks are you that I should ask your permission?"

"I am the fuck who you have fucked?"

(Dr. John Hopes starts the car and drives it on the road, and then Joan Banks smiles and asks Dr. John Hopes)

"You did not answer my question you fucking bastard?"

"If only I had known what a filthy whore you are? I wouldn't have even spit on you?"

"You called me a whore?"

"Yes I did?"

(Dr. John hopes is driving his car too fast, Joan Banks gets angry and moves her hand towards Dr. John Hopes, and then she says)

"You bastard, I will scratch your face?"

(Dr. John Hopes takes his hand away from the steering wheel to hold Joan Banks hand, Joan Banks hands touch the steering wheel and the car takes a left turn and bangs straight in to a big tree)

(Helen, Rosalie, Jane and Martha are sitting on the dining table having their dinner, and then Jane asks Helen)

"I heard that in the operation theatre Dr. John Hopes was very nervous?"

(Helen says)

"Yes, he was sweating so much and his hands were shaking too? I really felt sorry for him?"

(Martha gets angry, and then she says)

"Sorry for what he did to you Helen?

(Helen says)

"Martha, we are all human beings, as a doctor, he is still the best?"

(The house phone bell rings, Jane gets up and picks up the receiver of the phone, and then she says)

"Yes?"

(Jane hears the words from the other side and her face goes pale, and then she says)

"What! Oh my god?"

(The receiver of the phone slips down from the hand of Jane on to the floor, Helen, Rosalie and Martha get up from the chair and run towards Jane, and then Helen asks Jane)

"Jane! What's wrong?"

(Jane is trying to say something, but words don't come out of her mouth, and then Helen says)

"Please get some water?"

(Martha runs towards the dining table and picks up the glass of water and comes running towards Jane, Rosalie picks up the receiver of the phone and takes the receiver towards her ear, and then Rosalie says)

"The phone is disconnected?"

(Martha gives the glass of water to Jane, Jane drinks the water, then she starts crying, Helen takes Jane in her arms and tells her)

"Ok, ok, relax Jane"

(Jane wipes her tears, and then she says)

"There was a car accident of Dr. John Hopes' car?"

(Helen says)

"Oh no?"

(Jane starts crying, and then she says)

"The chief was on the phone, he said the lady sitting beside Dr. John Hopes was Joan Banks and she has died in the accident"

(Helen held both the hands of Jane with her hands, and then she asks)

"And Dr. John Hopes?"

"He has survived the accident but?"

(Helen shakes Jane with her hands, and then she asks)

"What Jane?"

(Jane again starts crying, and then she controls her crying and says)

"Both his legs are smashed to pieces"

(Helen starts crying, Rosalie and Martha also start crying, and then after a few seconds Jane says)

"We have to go to the hospital?"

(All four of them control their tears, Jane takes the keys of the car from the dining table, they all go out of the door, and then Martha closes the door behind her)

(Sharon is at the reception counter of the hospital; she is wiping her tears with a paper napkin, the phone bell rings, and then Sharon picks up the receiver of the phone and says)

"Get-well hospital, can I help you?"

(Sharon listens to the words from the other side, and then she says)

"Look, Dr. Robert Stanford is in the operation theatre, one of our doctors has met with an accident, ok, I'll give him the message when he comes out of the operation theatre"

(Sharon places the receiver on the phone, Helen, Jane, Rosalie and Martha come running, Helen comes near Sharon and then she asks her)

"Sharon how is Dr. John Hopes?"

(Sharon starts crying, Helen goes and holds Sharon in her arms, and then Sharon says)

"From knee downwards, the doctors are going to cut off both the legs of Dr. John Hopes"

(Helen leaves Sharon, and then she bangs her hand on her head and says)

"Oh my god?"

(Helen starts crying, Jane goes and takes Helen in her arms, and then Jane asks Sharon)

"Otherwise, Dr. John Hopes is ok?"

(Sharon wipes her tears, and then she says)

"He is hurt a little at the left side of his neck and some of his ribs are broken, but he seems ok because he was the one who called up Dr. Robert Stanford from his mobile phone"

(Jane looks up, and then she says)

"Thank god?"

(Tora Banks and Fred banks with tears running down their cheeks come running near the reception counter, and then Tora Banks asks)

"Where is my daughter Joan?"

(Sharon comes out from the reception counter, and then she tells Tora Banks)

"Come ma'am, I'll take you there?"

(Sharon takes Tora banks with her, Fred Banks comes near Helen, and then he asks)

"You are Helen?"

"Yes?"

"I know my daughter is no more? But still I am saying sorry to you?"

"That's ok sir"

"If I had been the man of the house? My daughter would have been alive today?"

"Extremely sorry about your daughter Mr. Fred Banks?"

"Everything was time pass for her, but today her time has come and she passed away?"

(Fred Banks starts crying, and then turns and walks away slowly, and then Helen says)

"Poor father, it must very hard to loose a daughter?"

(Bob and his wife Madeleine come there, and then Bob says)

"Any news about Dr. John Hopes?"

(Jane says)

"He is in the operating theatre and nobody has come out of the operation theatre?"

"Ok, I'll go and open the canteen, Madeleine come with me?"

(Bob and Madeleine go away, Dr. Mike Tyler and Jane's mother Carol come running, Jane sees them and then she asks)

"You two came very fast?"

(Dr. Mike Tyler tells Jane)

"The chief had made a call to me long time back?"

"Oh?"

(Dr. Mike Tyler goes away running towards the corridor of the hospital, and then Carol says)

"God has been kind to Dr. John Hopes, let's sit down on the sofa and pray for him?"

(Carol, Helen, Martha and Jane go towards the sofa and sit down on it, then all four fold their hands and starts praying)

AFTER ELEVEN MONTHS

(Dr. Robert Stanford has given a party at his house, Dr. John Hopes is on the wheel chair, Helen and Martha are standing together, Rosalie is with Wisdom, Jane who is six months pregnant is standing with her husband Dr. Mike Tyler and Carol, Bob is with his wife Madeleine, everybody has a glass in there hands, and then Dr. Robert Stanford raises his glass and then he says)

"This toast is for Dr. John Hopes"

(Everyone raises his or her glasses and touches their glass with each other glasses, tears comes in the eyes of Dr. John hopes, and then he says)

"Thank you everyone for your prayers and support to me?"

(Everyone says together)

"You are welcome"

(Dr. John Hopes smiles, and then he says)

"Rosalie you married Wisdom? Jane is six months pregnant?"

(Dr. Robert Stanford says)

"Dr. John Hopes, you should specially thank Helen for taking so much care of you when you were in the hospital?"

(Dr. John Hopes says)

"Helen, I salute you"

(Dr. John hopes puts his right hand on right side of his head, and then Dr. John Hopes says)

"Helen I am invalid? But if ever I can be of any help to you? I will be very happy?"

(Helen smiles, and then she says)

"Ok? Dr. John Hopes whatever I tell you? Will you swear upon god that you will do it?

"I swear upon god"

(Helen sits down in front of Dr. John Hopes and tells him)

"Then get married to me?"

(Everyone looks at Helen surprised, and then Dr. John Hopes asks)

"Helen! Think again what you have said just now?"

(Helen smiles, and then she says)

"I always think first? And then I say whatever I have to say?"

(Dr. John Hopes holds the hands of Helen, and then he tells her)

"But Helen?"

(Helen tells Dr. John Hopes)

"You swore upon god?"

"Why would you want to marry an invalid person like me?"

(Helen looks into the eyes of Dr. John Hopes, and then she tells him)

"Because love is eternal, it never dies"

(Dr. John Hopes looks at everyone, all of them shake their heads in a yes gesture, and Dr. John Hopes thinks for sometime, tears rolling down his eyes, and then he says)

"Ok"

(Everyone claps and they hug Helen and Dr. John hopes, and then Dr. Robert Stanford says)

"John, take good care of Helen after you marry her? Because now a days god does not make women like Helen?"

(Helen is shy, she says)

"Chief, you are embarrassing me?"

(Dr. Robert Stanford says)

"Helen, what is true is true? You can't hide it?"

(Carol puts her hand up, and then she says)

"I want to say something?"

(Dr. Robert Stanford says)

"Go ahead Carol? We are all ears?"

(Carol says)

"My dream is that we all live in one house Dr. Robert Stanford?"

(Dr. Robert Stanford looks at everyone, and then he says)

"I agree? Do you all agree?"

(Everyone says together)

"Yes we all agree"

(Carol says)

"Then it is decided, we buy a big house and stay together"

(In the church, Helen and Dr. John Hopes are getting married, Dr. John Hopes is on wheel chair, standing opposite him is Helen, and then the Priest asks Dr. John Hopes)

"Do you take this lady as your wedded wife?"

(Dr. John Hopes looks lovingly at Helen, and then he says)

"Yes I do"

(Then the priest asks Helen)

"Do you take this man as your wedded husband?"

(Helen says)

"Yes I do"

(The priest says)

"I now pronounce you man and wife"

(Everyone in the church claps, and then the priest tells Dr. John Hopes)

"You may kiss your bride"

(Helen goes towards Dr. John hopes, and then she bends down on her knees, Dr. John Hopes puts his lips on the lips of Helen)

The End.